1980

The First Cities

Series edited by Paul Johnstone and Anna Ritchie

The
First Cities

Ruth
Whitehouse

PHAIDON · OXFORD
E. P. DUTTON · NEW YORK

To John

Phaidon Press Limited, Littlegate House, St Ebbe's Street, Oxford
Published in the United States of America by E. P. Dutton

First published 1977

ISBN: hardback 0 7148 1678 7
       paperback 0 7148 1724 4
Library of Congress Catalog Card Number: 76-62640

Filmset in Great Britain by BAS Printers Limited, Wallop, Hampshire

Printed by Amilcare Pizzi SpA, Milan

Contents

90213

Erbil in present-day Iraq presents the mound, town wall and clustered mud-brick houses that would have characterized the world's first cities.

Chapter 1 Cities and Civilization

What is a city?
This book is entitled 'The First Cities' and its subject is the earliest cities
in the world: those that were built in the late fourth and third millennia BC
in a restricted area of western Asia. In writing about these early cities I
hope to do two things: to recreate what the cities were like and then
to explain how and why the first cities developed. These two aims reflect
the dual concerns of archaeology today, on the one hand to reconstruct
long-dead societies from their material remains and on the other to
explain the processes of man's past development.

Before we go any further we must discuss what we mean by 'city'.
Today we all live in an urban society and when we use terms like 'city',
'town' and 'village' we refer to such a society. If this sounds contradictory,
just reflect for a moment on the following facts. You may be living in a
tiny hamlet or isolated farm congratulating yourself on your escape from
urban pollution, but your retreat, however idyllic, is essentially a rural
component of an urban society. The wheat fields outside your window
produce flour for the towns and cities of the land; the milk from your
cows, the eggs that your hens lay, the bacon from your pigs, all go to
the nearest town or perhaps to the metropolis itself to be processed and
distributed. Conversely, your electricity and gas, your water supply and
your sewage disposal system are organized and brought to you from the
same urban centres. Here and there may flourish, perversely, an isolated
self-sufficient community, run by ex-city-dwellers in pursuit of ideological
purity; with love and faith one can run such a community, but as a valid
economic unit it has no meaning in a modern society. This is what I
mean when I say that we live in an urban society. When we use terms such
as 'town' or 'city' we do so in the context of a social organization which
includes, as units of settlement, villages, towns and cities, graduating in
size and complexity of organization. The definitions used by modern

demographers and urban geographers all reflect this fact. For instance, to distinguish between villages and towns simple numerical population values are often used: in Denmark a settlement with more than 200 people counts as a town, while in Greece one needs 10,000 people to qualify. Other authorities employ an economic criterion, often in combination with a numerical one: in India a town is a settlement of more than 5,000 people, of whom less than 25 per cent of the adult male population are engaged in agriculture. As for the distinction between 'town' and 'city', many authorities refuse to make an arbitrary division along what they consider to be a graduating series. When definitions are made, it is generally felt that simple numbers are irrelevant and economic and social criteria are used. To Jane Jacobs a city is 'a settlement that consistently generates its economic growth from its own local economy'. In Britain we somewhat quaintly call any town a city if it possesses a cathedral—with the result that we sometimes award a community the status that it had in the Middle Ages, when in reality such glories are only memories.

For the purpose of this book, however, we need some different definitions. We are talking of a time when the very first towns and cities came into existence. Before this there were settlements that we may describe as hamlets, villages or, occasionally, towns, but they had a fundamentally different nature from the units we designate by these names in our own society. Instead of representing steps in a graded series of communities forming part of a single economic system, they were (at least in theory) economically self-sufficient units, linked to no larger settlements and part of no larger economic system. But while prehistorians do use the terms 'hamlet', 'village' and sometimes—illogically, I think— 'town' in this non-urban context, they normally reserve the term 'city' exclusively for urban societies. The 'city' is the major unit of settlement of societies that have achieved the degree of organization that we describe as civilization. The terms 'city' and 'civilization' indeed share the same Latin root and show how closely associated the two concepts have long been in people's minds. It is in this sense that I use the term 'city' here. To attempt to define more precisely the 'city' is pointless; it is 'civilization' itself we must define.

Generally speaking we all know what we mean by civilization, but when we attempt a precise definition we run into difficulties: it is hard to find a definition that includes all those societies which by common consent are civilized and excludes all those which clearly are not. For the prehistorian dealing with past societies there are additional problems in the fact that the criteria most appropriate for defining civilization are not necessarily those that are easily recognized in the archaeological record. Thus prehistorians often use one set of criteria in general discussion and quite a different set to help them identify actual examples of civilized societies from the archaeological evidence. And of course it is quite possible that, in reference to particular societies, the two sets of criteria do not entirely coincide!

Some authorities are concerned with civilization as a particularly complex manifestation of human culture. The anthropologist A. L. Kroeber defined civilization as a particular pattern of culture with '. . . no distinctions of kind between civilization and culture'. Recently Colin Renfrew produced a definition along similar lines when he described civilization as '. . . the complex artificial environment of man; it is the insulation created by man, an artefact which mediates between himself and the world of nature'.

Other authorities emphasize the development of society. To Marxists the development of urban civilization represents the emergence of a class society. Marx himself, without any knowledge of archaeological data, conceived the development of society in its prehistoric past in three stages: (1) the nomadic community of hunter-gatherers; (2) the tribal community with permanent farming settlements, economically self-sufficient; and (3) the primary State with a class-structured community and concentrated settlement in towns. Gordon Childe, the eminent prehistorian, took over the Marxist model and adapted it to the evidence of archaeology. His particular contribution was to pinpoint the crucial significance of the periods of transition between the stages, which he labelled 'revolutions'. The first of Childe's revolutions, the 'Neolithic' or 'Food-producing' Revolution is concerned with the development of farming and had been accomplished in western Asia between six and four thousand years before the period covered by this book. Childe's second revolution, the 'Urban' Revolution, however, forms precisely the subject with which we *are* concerned here: the transformation of, in his own words '. . . some tiny villages of self-sufficing farmers into populous cities, nourished by secondary industries and foreign trade and regularly organized as States'. Most prehistorians today deprecate the use of the term 'revolution' to describe this change (or the earlier one), as it seems to have been a relatively slow and gradual process. However, the changes wrought in society were both fundamental and irreversible and to me at least it still seems apposite to describe them as revolutionary.

The Marxist model now seems too simple, but I still believe that we are right to look for the significance of the emergence of civilization in economic and social terms. Another scholar currently working on the problem of the origin of cities is Robert Adams and he too defines civilization in social terms. To him a civilized society is characterized by an interrelated set of social institutions: class stratification, political and religious hierarchies and the complex division of labour with full-time specialists of various sorts—a definition which is not out of line with the classical Marxist position.

For the prehistorian the problem is to recognize these institutions from the archaeological record. A number of attempts have been made to produce a definition that is applicable to archaeological data. The simplest and probably the most useful is that of Claude Kluckhohn who suggested that civilized societies must have two of the following three features: (a) towns of more than 5,000 people; (b) a written language; and (c) monumental ceremonial centres. At first sight this definition appears far too simple to be useful, but in practice it works quite well: certainly it includes all the societies that everyone agrees were civilized and excludes those prehistoric societies characterized by a single exceptional or precocious trait (e.g. the society that produced the stone temples of Malta, which had neither towns nor writing). What we must remember, however, is that the characteristics chosen by Kluckhohn are not themselves of overriding importance, though of course they *are* important, but are chosen because they are accessible to archaeologists. They are useful because they do seem to indicate the existence of the kind of social and economic structure by which Childe or Adams would define civilization, the emergence of which is the really important achievement of the Urban Revolution.

The 'first cities' of this book's title are the settlements of the earliest civilizations that arose in the world and it is with these civilizations, their character and their origins, that we are concerned. They developed in the late fourth and the third millennia BC in parts of western Asia and north Africa. The three large alluvial systems of the Tigris-Euphrates, the Nile and the Indus supported three great ancient civilizations. Of these, that of Mesopotamia (first the Sumerian and later the Babylonian and Assyrian) is both the earliest in origin and in many ways the best understood, accessible through archaeology and through written documents. In addition, unlike the mute testimonies of the Harappan civilization of the Indus Valley (for the Indus script is still undeciphered) or the impressive but inward-looking traditions of the Egyptians, Mesopotamian culture does not appear entirely alien to us today. Though separated from us by four thousand years or more, the inheritance of ancient Sumer can still be recognized in our own traditions—and I am writing now of specific traits of Sumerian culture, not of general technological achievements which *may* have been made first by the Sumerians but which were probably invented in and diffused from numerous centres at different times. Because many of the practices and beliefs of Sumer were passed on to the Babylonians and Assyrians and thence, through contact and deliberate borrowing, to the Hittites, the Phoenicians and finally the Greeks, some reached our own cultural heritage. And at a later date Christianity also acted as an agent of diffusion, bringing religious ideas rooted in the ancient East into the Roman world and our culture. Specific traits that we can trace back to Sumer include, in the field of mathematics, positional numeration where the value of a number is determined by its position in a sequence of numbers (as in the decimal system), and the sexagesimal system by which we divide the clock and the circle and, in the religious sphere, the concept of the creative power of the divine word and the story of the Universal Flood. The latter was probably composed in the watery marshes of southern Mesopotamia on which Sumerian civilization was laboriously created.

Because of the earlier emergence of the Mesopotamian civilization, our relatively thorough understanding of it and its relevance to our own culture, I shall concentrate on it in this book. Ancient Egyptian civilization is the subject of another book in this series and will not be dealt with here, except in general discussion. I shall deal also, though secondarily, with the Harappan civilization of the Indus Valley as well as with other urban communities that arose elsewhere in western Asia: on the coasts and islands of the Persian Gulf, in valleys dissecting the Afghan and Iranian plateaux and in Turkmenia. I shall be concerned in the main with the early phases of these civilizations and in particular with their genesis.

The book is arranged in three parts. In the introductory section this chapter is followed by one devoted to the discovery of the early civilizations. The five chapters in part 2 are primarily descriptive: three deal with Mesopotamia, especially with the Sumerians; chapter 6 deals with the civilization of the Indus Valley and chapter 7 with the various smaller urban centres that grew up in other parts of western Asia. Part 3 of the book is concerned with explanation: chapter 8 provides the prehistoric background to the emergence of civilization; chapter 9 attempts to deal with the crucial questions of how and why civilization emerged and finally summarizes my main conclusions in a general discussion.

Dating the first cities
I hope to avoid involvement in the minutiae of discussion over chronology, a study which is best left to the pages of specialist journals. However it is necessary to provide some chronological framework and here I shall briefly mention some of the difficulties we have in dealing with a time-scale for the first civilizations of western Asia. The chief problem arises because we derive chronological information from two entirely different sources: the 'historical' chronology of Mesopotamia which is based on documentary sources and an independent 'archaeological' chronology derived from radiocarbon (C14) dates. There are separate internal problems in the interpretation of both these types of data and an additional problem in correlating the two sets of information.

The historical chronology of Mesopotamia, both in its early Sumerian and later Babylonian and Assyrian phases, is based on a series of 'King

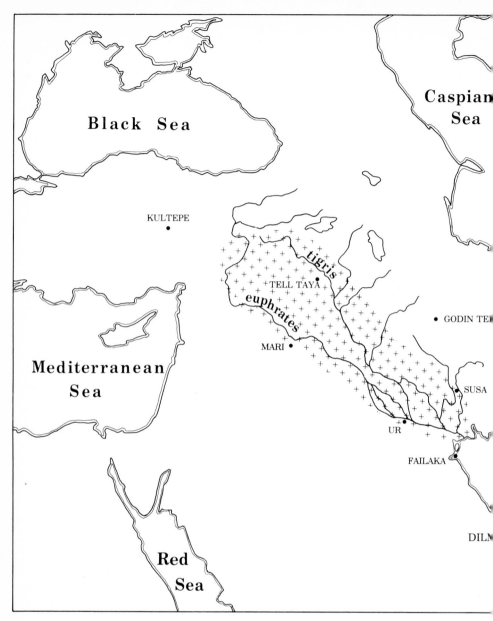

Areas on Tigris, Euphrates and Indus (shaded) where the first cities arose.

Lists' which represent the historical tradition of the land, purporting to enumerate all the kings that had reigned since the beginning of time. The 'Sumerian King List' is compiled from about fifteen documents, the earliest of which is dated to some time not long before 2000 BC; it is unlikely that they copy earlier documents, though they doubtless incorporate an oral tradition of considerable antiquity. The Sumerians and their

12

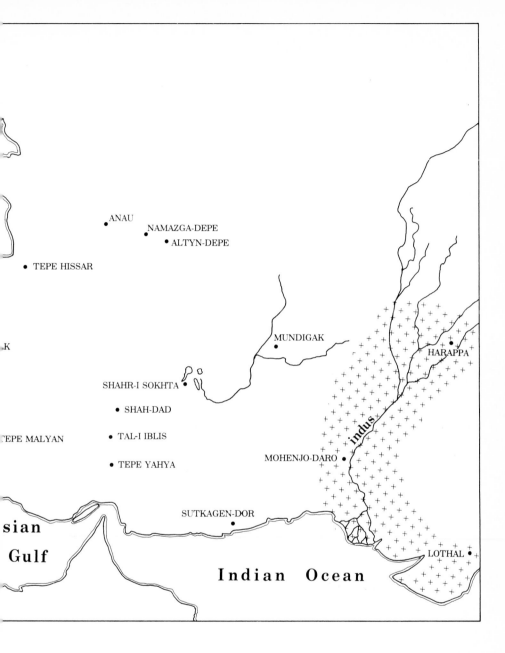

ANAU

NAMAZGA-DEPE

ALTYN-DEPE

TEPE HISSAR

MUNDIGAK

HARAPPA

SHAHR-I SOKHTA

SHAH-DAD

EPE MALYAN

TAL-I IBLIS

MOHENJO-DARO

TEPE YAHYA

indus

sian

Gulf

SUTKAGEN-DOR

LOTHAL

Indian Ocean

K

K

successors had an accurate calendar, so there are no problems in converting 'their' years to 'our' years. There are, however, other considerable problems in using the King List as a direct source of chronological reckoning. Its first part refers more to mythology than history, for it records a period 'before the Flood', during which eight (or possibly ten) kings reigned over a period of rather more than 240,000 years! The early post-diluvian kings are also credited with reigns of superhuman length, though much shorter than those of their antediluvian ancestors: the twenty-three kings of the First Dynasty of Kish, the first to rule after the Flood, are allotted 24,500 years in all. As the King List approaches the time at which it was compiled it becomes increasingly realistic and, where it can be checked against other information such as inscriptions on monuments, increasingly reliable. From the time of Sargon of Agade (about 2371–2316 BC or 2334–2279 BC depending on the interpretation of the documentary evidence) the dates are unlikely to be moved by more than half a century either way by the discovery of new documents or the reinterpretation of old ones. Before this the dates cannot be calculated with anything like this precision—partly because the King List exaggerates the length of reigns and partly because it lists dynasties of different cities as successive, whereas they may have been partly contemporary. As a result some scholars favour a 'long' and others a 'short' chronology: the earliest estimates for the beginning of the Early Dynastic period fall in about 3200 BC, the latest in about 2800 BC. What is clear is that for this period we must not convince ourselves that we have a precise chronology based on historical documents.

Radiocarbon provides a method of dating archaeological material that is entirely independent of historical documents. It depends on the fact that C14, a radioactive component of carbon which is found in all organic materials, starts decaying at the moment the organism dies and that the rate of decay is both known and measurable. However, in the last few years a problem has arisen over radiocarbon dating. When an extremely long-lived type of tree, the bristlecone pine (*Pinus aristata*), was discovered in the Californian mountains, attempts were made to check radiocarbon dates against the calendar provided by dendro-chronology (counting of the annual growth rings of the trees). The result of this calibration demonstrated that 'radiocarbon years' have differed in length from 'real' calendar years by different amounts at different periods in the past, with a maximum recorded divergence of 800–900 years in the fifth millennium BC (we cannot at present calibrate radiocarbon dates earlier than about 4300 BC). The tree-ring calibration of radiocarbon dates is still not accepted by all prehistorians and certainly the calibration charts will have to be altered in detail as work progresses; however, in general, the corrected dates fit historical chronologies much better than do un-corrected dates. A series of radiocarbon dates obtained from historically datable contexts in Egypt was run specifically for the purpose of checking the relative accuracies of the uncorrected radiocarbon calendars and those calibrated with tree rings. In almost every case the radiocarbon date calibrated with tree rings was in closer agreement with the historical date than the uncorrected one. Unfortunately no comparable sequence is available for Mesopotamia, but there are three radiocarbon dates for the Royal Graves at Ur; these have an average of 2030 ± 100 bc, which gives a mean calibrated date of about 2500 BC. The Royal Graves of Ur belong to the Early Dynastic III period of Sumer, which came to an end in about 2370 BC in the historical chronology; thus, in this case too, the calibrated chronology fits better than the uncorrected radiocarbon dates.

In this book I shall have to use both 'historical' and 'archaeological' dates. I shall follow the current British usage and use the small letters bc for uncorrected radiocarbon dates. The small capitals BC will be used both for calibrated radiocarbon dates and for historical dates—in other words for all dates which are thought to be 'real' dates in calendar years. Where it is necessary to know whether a date is a historical one or a corrected radiocarbon one, I shall make it clear in the text. The chronology adopted here is a relatively long one: it is based on the radiocarbon chronology calibrated with tree rings for the period before about 2500 BC and, for the later period, on the long 'historical' chronology proposed initially by Professor Sidney Smith, which puts the beginning of Sargon of Agade's reign (and therefore the end of the Early Dynastic period) at 2371 BC. There is not enough evidence for us to feel certain of this chronology, but at present it seems to fit the evidence satisfactorily and is used as a general framework here.

Chapter II   The Discovery of the First Cities

The excitement of unearthing the unknown is part of the appeal of archaeology. Even today, when so much exploration and excavation has taken place, archaeologists can still make discoveries that cast a startling new light on man's past development, fill major gaps in the story of his achievement or add to the art treasures of the world. The anticipation of such a discovery, however little it may be expected, is an additional attraction in a study in which the main stimulus is the more rigorous intellectual appeal of a scientific discipline. If this excitement still moves us today, how much more exciting must have been the discovery of whole new and unsuspected civilizations? For, one hundred and fifty years ago, the civilizations described in this book were neither known nor guessed at. From the 1840s onwards the evidence for Sumerian civilization was extracted slowly and under conditions more hazardous than those facing any archaeologists today. The Indus Valley civilizations came to light only in the 1920s, while the discovery of the urban centres of the Persian Gulf, highland Iran and Turkmenia belong to the last twenty-five years. Indeed, important new discoveries are being made in this area yearly and there is little doubt that by the time this book is in print more than one new major site will have been found. In this chapter I shall concentrate on the Sumerian civilization whose discovery has many of the attributes of an adventure story and which cannot but arouse our admiration for the archaeologists and epigraphists to whose energy, fortitude and scholarship we owe so much of our knowledge of the world's first cities. I shall also describe briefly the discovery of the Indus Valley civilization and the towns of Turkmenia, Iran and the Persian Gulf and shall conclude with a brief discussion of the contribution to this field now being made by the techniques and approaches of modern archaeology.

Mesopotamia has always been known as the seat of ancient civilization through the Bible and through classical sources. Names such as Babylon,

The hazards of early archaeological exploration in Mesopotamia were well illustrated in Layard's report of his discoveries in the 1840s. ▶

Nineveh and Ur were familiar to all readers of the Old Testament and indeed the name of Sumer itself is probably enshrined there in the form of Shinar (Genesis XI). However, the extreme antiquity of this civilization was not recognized and, moreover, nothing was known about its nature beyond the references in biblical and classical literature. It was exactly comparable to the knowledge of Troy and Mycenae which was derived entirely from Homer until Schliemann's excavations of the 1870s and 1880s unearthed the cities themselves. Just as Schliemann discovered Mycenaean civilization, so his contemporaries in Mesopotamia discovered first the Babylonian and Assyrian civilizations and subsequently the Sumerian civilization with which we are above all concerned in this book.

Evidence for Mesopotamian civilization comes from two sources— archaeological and documentary—and these provided two separate avenues to understanding, followed by men of different disciplines, but leading to the same destination. As it happens these two avenues were opened up at approximately the same time. While archaeologists were unearthing buildings and artefacts, language scholars were deciphering inscriptions written in the strange cuneiform script which they found initially on standing stone monuments in Iran but which they soon recognized also on clay tablets excavated in thousands from the buried cities of Mesopotamia. The archaeological contribution to our knowledge of Mesopotamian civilization was a steady build-up of information, gaining in complexity and extending further back in time as the excavations progressed. The linguistic contribution, by contrast, although also based on a steady accumulation of hard work, took the form of a number of major break-throughs, and pride of place in this account must go to the decipherment of the various languages of Mesopotamia and Iran written in the cuneiform script. It was these that opened the door to the under- standing of the later Mesopotamian civilizations (Babylon and Assyria) and subsequently to the recognition of the unsuspected earlier civilization of Sumer.

Decipherment of the languages
On a number of sites in Iran there are trilingual inscriptions, carved in the Achaemenian period (mid-first millennium BC) on stone monuments and mountain sides. There are important inscriptions at Persepolis (Takht-i Jamshid), the neighbouring site of Naqsh-i Rustam and on Mount Elvend near Hamadan, but the most important of all is at Behistun (or Bisitun, as it is more often transcribed today) near Kermanshah. Here an area of the rock face covering more than 100 square metres, more than 100 metres above ground level, had been specially prepared and inscribed with a trilingual text many hundreds of lines long. The three languages that figure in the Persian trilinguals are Babylonian (now known as

Woolley's excavations in the 1920s revealed the great height of the ascent to the shrine on the ziggurat at Ur.

Akkadian), Elamite and Old Persian. They were all three written in the cuneiform script and both the script itself and all three languages were unknown to scholars at the beginning of the nineteenth century. Thus the task facing the would-be decipherers of these languages was much more daunting than that tackled by the scholars of ancient Egypt who had, on the Rosetta Stone, one completely understood text in Greek to provide a key for the decipherment of ancient Egyptian.

The key to the decipherment of the Mesopotamian languages proved to lie in the Old Persian inscriptions. Fortunately very ancient Persian writings, known as the Zend-Avesta, have been preserved by the small Zoroastrian communities of Iran and India up to the present day and are so close to the language of the Old Persian inscriptions that they share many words with exactly the same sound and meaning. These words allowed scholars to decipher Old Persian in what Cyrus Gordon has called the 'hard way'—without the aid of bilingual inscriptions. After the decipherment of Old Persian, it could be used to help decipher the other two languages of the trilingual inscriptions: Elamite and Babylonian (Akkadian).

The first successful decipherment of Old Persian was by a German teacher, Georg Friedrich Grotefend, who presented a paper to the Göttingen Academy in 1802; unfortunately the Academy refused to publish it and Grotefend's work was largely ignored. The credit for producing the first recognized decipherment of Old Persian, as well as making major contributions towards the decipherment of both Elamite and Babylonian, must go to the Englishman Henry Creswicke Rawlinson (1810–1895), a colonel in the Indian army who became British Resident and Consul-General in Baghdad. It was Rawlinson who took on the incredible task of transcribing the Bisitun trilingual inscription. Between 1835 and 1837 he copied about 200 of the 414 lines of the Old Persian text. The Old Persian inscription was the most accessible of the three, but even this had to be reached by ropes and ladders. In Rawlinson's own words: '. . . even with ladders there is considerable risk, for the foot-ledge is so narrow, about eighteen inches or at most two feet in breadth . . . the upper inscription can only be copied by standing on the topmost step of the ladder with no other support than steadying the body against the rock with the left arm, while the left hand holds the note-book and the right arm is employed with the pencil. In this position I copied all the upper inscriptions and the interest of the occupation entirely did away with any sense of danger'. Rawlinson's work at Bisitun was interrupted by the demands of his military career, but he returned in 1844 and finished the whole Old Persian inscription of 414 lines and the entire Elamite inscription of 263 lines. The 112 lines of the Babylonian version gave Rawlinson more trouble than either of the others and, indeed, he found the task of climbing up to it beyond even his considerable powers. Although

Decipherment of the Mesopotamian languages stemmed from Rawlinson's perilous climb up the rock face to record this tri-lingual inscription at Bisitun.

the inscription could be read from below with the aid of a telescope, Rawlinson wanted to take a paper 'squeeze' of it. This he finally achieved in 1847 with the help of a 'wild Kurdish boy' who managed to suspend a swinging seat in front of the vertical rock face and under Rawlinson's direction took a paper cast of the inscription which, in Rawlinson's words, 'is almost of equal value for the interpretation of the Assyrian inscriptions as was the Greek translation on the Rosetta Stone for the intelligence of the hieroglyphic texts of Egypt'.

Rawlinson was not satisfied with transcribing the inscriptions but was actively engaged on their decipherment also. By the late 1830s he had virtually completed the decipherment of the Old Persian script and started work on the Elamite version. However, although he had some success with this too, he realized before long that the decipherment of Elamite was less important than that of Babylonian (and so it has proved, for Elamite is both isolated linguistically and restricted geographically to the area of western Iran). He turned his attention to the Babylonian version and had more or less accomplished its decipherment by the middle of the century. Meanwhile a number of other distinguished scholars had been hard at work on the same problems. Chief among these were the Irishman Edward Hincks, the Frenchman Jules Oppert and the Englishman William Henry Fox Talbot. The success of their efforts was put to the test in a striking manner in 1857 when all four scholars happened to be in London. Each was given a copy of a cylinder of Tiglathpileser I that had only just been discovered, with instructions to work on it separately and to return their solutions in sealed envelopes—the whole operation supervised by the Royal Asiatic Society. The four translations turned out to agree in all essentials and the decipherment of Akkadian was generally recognized.

Until at least the 1840s not even the chief scholars suspected that the cuneiform script had not been invented by the Babylonians at all but by a people speaking an entirely different language that we now know as Sumerian. It was Hincks, in 1850, who first voiced suspicions on this subject and a further contribution was made two years later by Rawlinson who recognized that some of the tablets found at Kuyunjik (one of the mounds covering the ruins of ancient Nineveh) were bilingual word-lists. One of the languages was the by now familiar Babylonian and the other was Sumerian, which, however, Rawlinson first labelled Scythic and later, confusingly, Akkadian (the name which is now applied to Babylonian). It was Oppert who suggested in 1869 that this language should be called Sumerian, accurately extracting the correct name from the title 'King of Sumer and Akkad' (now often transcribed 'Agade') found on some early inscriptions. Furthermore he recognized the distinctive structure of the Sumerian language and correctly compared it to Turkish and to the Finno-Ugrian languages. In the last twenty-five years of the nineteenth century Sumerian tablets came to light in large numbers on the excavations at Lagash and Nippur and, by the turn of the century, the decipherment of Sumerian had been more or less fully accomplished.

The decipherment of the languages was only the beginning of the story. Since then the cumulative efforts of many cuneiform scholars over the years has gradually built up for us a picture, though very far from a complete one, of the ancient Mesopotamian civilizations. Most of these efforts were unrewarding in the short term, producing fragments of information that made little or no sense by themselves, only to fall into place eventually in a vast jigsaw made up of innumerable similar scraps of information (some of which, of course, will probably never be found). There are exceptions however: occasionally discoveries are made that are of outstanding interest in themselves. One can imagine, for instance, the public excitement engendered in 1872 when an amateur scholar of cuneiform called George Smith (who had been a bank-note engraver by profession) announced that, in working through the tablets from Assurbanipal's library in Nineveh, now held by the British Museum, he had come across part of a Babylonian version of the biblical Flood story. I shall quote part of the story here, to show the similarities to the Old Testament account. Here, the Noah figure, Uta-Napishtim, has built his boat and is about to embark:

'What I had, I loaded thereon, the whole harvest of life
I caused to embark within the vessel; all my family and relations,
The beasts of the field, the cattle of the field, the craftsmen,
    I made them all embark.
I entered the vessel and closed the door . . .
When the young dawn gleamed forth
From the foundations of heaven a black cloud arose;
Adad roared in it,
Nabu and the King march in front . . .
Nergal seizeth the mast,
He goeth, Inurta leadeth the attack . . .
The tumult of Adad ascends to the skies.
All that is bright is turned into darkness,
The brother seeth the brother no more,
The folk of the skies can no longer recognize each other.
The gods feared the flood,
They fled, they climbed into the heaven of Anu,
The gods crouched like a dog on the wall, they lay down . . .
For six days and nights
Wind and flood marched on, the hurricane subdued the land.
When the seventh day dawned the hurricane was abated, the flood
Which had waged war like an army;

The sea was stilled, the ill wind was calmed, the flood ceased.
I beheld the sea, its voice was silent
And all mankind was turned into mud!
As high as the roofs reached the swamp! . . .
I beheld the world, the horizon of sea;
Twelve measures away an island emerged;
Unto mount Nitsir came the vessel,
Mount Nitsir held the vessel and let it not budge . . .
When the seventh day came
I sent forth a dove, I released it;
It went, the dove, it came back,
As there was no place, it came back.
I sent forth a swallow, I released it;
It went, the swallow, it came back,
As there was no place, it came back.
I sent forth a crow, I released it;
It went, the crow, and beheld the subsidence of the waters;
It eats, it splashes about, it caws, it comes not back.'

In 1872 the public reacted with astonishment as, for the first time, an Old Testament story was seen as part of a much wider western Asiatic tradition. This idea is commonplace now, but then it was unfamiliar and to many people unacceptable. The story made newspaper headlines at the time and, indeed, the *Daily Telegraph* offered Smith 1,000 guineas to go to Nineveh himself to find the part of the story that was still missing. Smith made the trip in the spring of 1873 and within a matter of days found a fragment, seventeen lines long, which filled the only serious gap in the British Museum account—the kind of success story of which every archaeologist dreams! Since that time other versions of the Flood story have become available, including a Sumerian version in which the Noah figure is called Ziusudra, in place of the Uta-Napishtim of the Akkadian version: there is now little doubt of the ultimate Sumerian origin of the Old Testament Flood story.

If George Smith's discovery of the Flood story in Assurbanipal's library was the most spectacular of all cuneiform 'finds', other exciting discoveries have followed. One such discovery was that by Samuel Kramer of the law-code of Ur-nammu, first king of the Third Dynasty of Ur, some three centuries earlier than the famous code of Hammurabi. Nor are the possibilities of new exciting discoveries remote: only a small proportion of all the cuneiform tablets already excavated have been translated and the soil of Mesopotamia undoubtedly covers many thousands more. From the point of view of work to be done, we are still at the beginning of the story.

24

Archaeological excavation in Mesopotamia

We must now turn from the scholars who studied the ancient documents to the archaeologists, to men such as Botta, Layard, Place and Loftus, no less intrepid than Rawlinson, who braved solitude, illness and immense practical difficulties in their efforts to unearth the ancient cities themselves. Excavation began in the 1840s when P. E. Botta, the French consular agent at Mosul, started digging at Nineveh and the Englishman Henry Layard at Nimrud. The following decade saw excavations by two other Englishmen, in this case in the extreme southern part of ancient Sumer: W. K. Loftus at Uruk (modern Warka, Biblical Erech) and T. E. Taylor at Ur and at Eridu. The two most important excavations of the last quarter of the nineteenth century were also both on Sumerian sites. The French consul in Basra excavated ancient Lagash (modern Telloh) intermittently from 1877 until the end of the century. The other site was Nippur, which was excavated by an American team from the University of Pennsylvania between 1889 and 1900 under several different directors, including finally the noted Assyriologist H. V. Hilprecht. These two sites— Lagash and Nippur—have yielded by far the largest number of Sumerian tablets we have; the four seasons' work at Nippur alone unearthed about thirty thousand tablets or fragments, mostly in the Sumerian language.

The quality of nineteenth-century excavation in Mesopotamia, as in most other parts of the world, was by modern standards appalling. The overriding motive for the work was the collection of material for museums —cuneiform tablets and *objets d'art*—and this often took the form of what Seton Lloyd described in one case as 'an undignified scramble for archaeological loot'. The principle of stratigraphy, the foundation of scientific excavation, was largely ignored and the recording of both deposits and buildings was inadequate or non-existent. Moreover the progress of the study was hindered by unseemly squabbles over the right of a particular excavator to a particular site, battles usually fought on nationalist lines. Sir Wallis Budge described the situation at Nineveh where 'Layard continued to open trenches on the south side of the mound and the French consul went on digging little pits a few feet deep in another direction'. This is one side of the picture, but there is also the other, already mentioned, to which we must pay tribute. The conditions under which these early excavators worked were horrifyingly difficult: most of the sites could only be reached by several days' journey on mule-back from the urban centres of Mosul, Baghdad and Basra; all civilized facilities were consequently lacking; serious disease was prevalent. There were other hazards too: Hilprecht's excavations at Nippur were more than once threatened by hostile local tribesmen. The sufferings of individuals were great—on many levels, as we can see from this account by Layard of an experience he underwent in 1840: 'I had slept little, as I was suffering greatly from toothache. The sheikh declared that there was a skilful dentist

INDUS VALLEY				
PERSIAN GULF				
TURKMENIA				
SUSIANA	SUSA A		SUSA B	SUSA C
SOUTH MESOPOTAMIA UBAID *Early Ubaid*	*Late Ubaid*	URUK *Early Uruk*	*Late Uruk*	PROTO-LITERATE (Jamdat Nasr
6000 BC	5000 BC		4000 BC	

A time-table of the emergence of the first civilizations. (1=Akkadian period, 2=The Guti, 3=Third Dynasty of Ur.)

in the encampment, and as the pain was almost unbearable, I made up my mind to put myself in his hands rather than endure it any longer. He was accordingly sent for. He was a tall, muscular Arab. His instruments consisted of a short knife or razor, and a kind of iron awl. He bade me sit on the ground, and then took my head firmly between his knees. After cutting away at the gums he applied the awl to the roots of the tooth, and, striking the other end with all his might, expected to see the tooth fly into the air. The awl slipped and made a severe wound in my palate. He insisted upon a second trial, declaring that he could not but succeed. But the only result was that he broke off a large piece of the tooth, and I had suffered sufficient agony to decline a third experiment.' No twentieth-century excavator is called upon to undergo quite that kind of ordeal!

In the twentieth century the study of the ancient Mesopotamian civilizations came of age and the time of the great pioneers was over. Much progress remained to be made, it is true: archaeological techniques on most excavations were still grossly inadequate and on the language side the complexities and ambiguities of the cuneiform script meant that the sense of many tablets continued to elude even the most proficient scholars. However the foundation of the study had been laid and it remained for twentieth-century scholars to build on this foundation.

In the first half of the present century excavations began on many of the most important cities of Sumer. The first decade of the century saw the German excavation at Shuruppak (modern Fara) and the University

26

Great age of pyramid building in Egypt
First phase of building at Stonehenge
Earliest civilization in China (Shang)

								BIRTH OF CHRIST
RE-ARAPPAN	HARAPPAN							
	DILMUN							
AMAZGA IV	NAMAZGA V							
JSA D								
YNASTIC D.I E.D II E.D.III		1	2	3	ISIN & LARSA	OLD BABYLONIAN		
00 BC				2000 BC		1000 BC		

of Chicago's expedition to Adab (modern Bismaya). The site of Kish was excavated first by a French expedition in 1912–14 and later by an Anglo-American team from 1923 to 1932. A German expedition excavated at Uruk both before and after World War II. The sounding in the Eanna sanctuary at Uruk, which descended approximately twenty metres to virgin soil, has provided a crucial stratigraphy for the prehistoric period in southern Mesopotamia, from a level dated to about 5000 BC (Uruk XVIII) to a level of the mid-fourth millennium BC (Uruk V) at the top of the sounding, which was the court of the so-called Limestone Temple. Elsewhere on the site late prehistoric and 'Protoliterate' (Uruk IV–I) and Early Dynastic levels were excavated.

Undoubtedly the most spectacular and among the most important excavations ever conducted in Mesopotamia took place in the 1920s under the direction of Leonard Woolley (later Sir Leonard Woolley) who led a joint expedition of the British Museum and the University Museum of Pennsylvania. Woolley was a skilful excavator for his time; moreover he was an extremely lucky one. As well as excavating many important buildings in the city, including the vast *ziggurat* (staged temple tower) of Ur-nammu, founder of the Third Dynasty of Ur, he also made a number of spectacular finds. One of the important discoveries made by his expedition was the small but splendidly decorated shrine dedicated to the goddess Ninhursag on the site of al'Ubaid, six kilometres north-west of Ur (the same site that has given its name to the main prehistoric culture

27

of southern Mesopotamia). This temple produced a dedicatory inscription which included the name of a king who appears in the Sumerian King List as a ruler of the First Dynasty of Ur. Until this discovery scholars had tended to regard the First Dynasty of Ur as legendary; Woolley's discovery marked a turning point in the acceptance of the King List as at least a partially valid historical document.

However, the discovery which brought the Sumerians into the light of day as far as the general public was concerned, and for which Woolley himself is best remembered, was that of the Royal Cemetery at Ur, which he found in 1922 and excavated between 1926 and 1931. The discovery of these monumental tombs with their magnificent grave furniture of gold, silver and lapis lazuli and their evidence of human sacrifice, in the form of the king's retinue buried with the royal dead, had an enormous impact on the public. If the names of kings Mes-kalam-dug and A-kalam-dug and queen Shub-ad (as she used to be called; nowadays she is usually read as Pu-abi) have never become household words like those of Tutan-khamun and Nefertiti, it was nonetheless the discovery of their tombs that brought to the public some understanding of the world's earliest civilization.

The 1930s saw important American excavations in the Diyala area, led by Henri Frankfort. The settlement mounds or tells of Asmar, Khafaje and Agrab, though north-east of Sumer proper, have yielded every bit as much information about Sumerian civilization as have the Sumerian cities of the far south. So indeed has the city of Mari, far to the north-west, on the middle Euphrates, which was excavated by the French, under André Parrot, continuously from 1933 to 1956, apart from an interruption during the war years. Here a city inhabited even in the earliest period by Semitic speakers was shown to have been virtually indistinguishable culturally from the southern Sumerian cities. The period of World War II saw the beginning of large-scale excavations by the Iraqis themselves. Of the several sites excavated by the Iraqi Directorate of Antiquities during the 1940s the most interesting was Eridu. Here Fuad Safar excavated the earliest settlement yet discovered in southern Mesopotamia, a series of religious buildings dedicated to the sea god Enki, and two early royal palaces of the mid-third millennium BC. In the post-war years most of the excavation has been done by the Iraqis. There have been only two foreign expeditions to the south, to Sumer proper: the Germans returned to Uruk and the Americans to Nippur. In northern Mesopotamia there have been many more foreign excavations, but most of these have been on prehistoric sites or on historical sites of much later periods. The most exciting excavation of the period with which we are concerned here is at Tell Taya, west of Mosul, where in the last few years the British, under Julian Reade, have planned large areas of and excavated parts of a big city of the Early Dynastic or Sargonid period. At Tell Taya, unlike most Mesopotamian sites, the building material was not mud-brick but stone. This fortunate occurrence, combined with the fact that Tell Taya's period of prosperity and maximum expansion seems to have been relatively short, has provided us with a unique opportunity of obtaining a more or less single-period plan of a mid-third millennium BC Mesopotamian city.

Discovery of the Indus civilization

As we have seen, the knowledge of ancient Mesopotamian civilization had always been part, however dimly perceived, of general knowledge—thanks to the Bible. By contrast the almost equally ancient civilization of the Indus Valley was completely unsuspected until it was uncovered by the archaeologists and that did not happen until the 1920s. A book entitled *The Antiquities of India* by Barrett, published in 1913, maintained that 'In India there is no twilight before the dark'. In fact the hints were there in the ancient sacred literature of India, just as references to Mesopotamian civilization occurred in the Bible, but these hints were discounted by most scholars. The hymns of the Rig-Veda, in the Sanskrit language, written down only in the eighteenth century AD but transmitted orally from very early times, describe the arrival of the *Aryas* (Aryan-speaking peoples) in India. They refer to the indigenous population which the *Aryas* found and conquered: they called them the *Dasus* and described them as skilled in various arts and as living in large and prosperous cities. Most scholars now accept that the *Dasus* were the people of the Indus Valley civilization and that the Rig-Veda preserves a faint memory of their achievements. Until the 1920s, however, the view that the pre-Aryan population of India was civilized, though occasionally expressed, met with general disbelief. So when in 1921 Sir John Marshall, Director General of Archaeology in India, excavated at not one but both of the great metropolises of the Indus civilization—Harappa in the Punjab and Mohenjo-Daro in Sind—he was unearthing a totally new civilization and presenting the world of scholarship with a totally new concept to be grappled with and absorbed. We now know that this was the most extensive of all the pre-classical civilizations and apparently the most highly organized.

Work continued on the Indus cities throughout the Twenties and Thirties, but we owe a very large part of our present knowledge of the civilization to the work of Sir Mortimer Wheeler, who became Director General of Archaeology in India in the 1940s. He excavated with all the skill and efficiency with which his name is associated and also wrote several valuable general works on the whole Indus civilization. Since partition of the country work has continued both in Pakistan (formerly West Pakistan) and in India and our knowledge of the civilization continues to grow.

The last thirty years

By the time of World War II scholars, and to some extent the general public also, had come to accept that there had existed in the third millennium BC three great civilizations in Egypt, Mesopotamia and the Indus Valley. Archaeologists had uncovered large areas of their cities, exposed the most impressive of their buildings and retrieved their greatest art treasures—to the permanent benefit of the famous museums of the world. Epigraphists had deciphered their languages (at least in the case of Egypt and Mesopotamia; the Indus script is still undeciphered) and had translated many of their writings. Moreover, a number of scholars, outstanding among whom were Henri Frankfort and Gordon Childe, grappled with the problems of the nature and origin of civilization itself. And, oversimplified as their accounts now seem, they have far from outlived their usefulness. Childe's *New Light on the Most Ancient East*, published in 1934, as a revision of a book published six years earlier entitled simply *The Most Ancient East*, and revised and reprinted many times since, is still a most valuable account.

In the years since the war, work has continued steadily on all these fronts and in new directions also. In spite of what I have just said about the continuing usefulness of Childe's account, the views that many scholars now hold about the nature and origins of western Asiatic civilization are very different from those expressed in *New Light on the Most Ancient East*, even in the later revisions. We owe our new views in part to new discoveries, in part to new techniques of excavation, recovery and analysis, but most of all to new attitudes. Archaeologists today are asking different questions from those asked thirty years ago and are therefore coming up with new interpretations.

New discoveries have altered our views on the ancient civilizations in two main ways: they have provided us with an ancestry and with a contemporary context for their development. The civilizations of Egypt, Mesopotamia and the Indus Valley no longer appear as isolated developments, outbursts of cultural creativity, appearing from nowhere and existing in geographical isolation. We can now document the background to the emergence of civilization in western Asia. Excavations in the last thirty years have shown us the gradual development of farming and the establishment of settled village communities over the highland zones of the Near East between 9000 and 6000 bc. They have shown us the beginnings of irrigation agriculture and the gradual spread of the expanding population on to the alluvial soils of the great river valleys between 6000 and 3000 bc. They have shown us the developing technology that enabled man to deal with this new environment. They have documented the still expanding population clustering into fewer larger settlements and the gradual emergence of the forms and functions of city life. Not only have the excavations of the post-war years provided us with the ancestors of the world's first city-dwellers: they have also shown us their neighbours. We now know that there were towns in the third millennium BC not only in the areas of the three main civilizations, but also in Turkmenia (Soviet central Asia), in highland Iran and Afghanistan and on the coasts and islands of the Persian Gulf. The relationship between the towns of these different areas provides one of the main subjects of study at the present.

New archaeological techniques have contributed to our knowledge in a number of different ways. In the first place we now collect much more information from archaeological excavations than we used to. This is partly the result of refining existing techniques and partly due to the invention of new ones. For instance, the new technique of flotating soil samples allows us to collect surviving plant remains from many kinds of deposit and to reconstruct the vegetable diet of past societies to a much greater degree than we were able to previously. Secondly, we can now examine the finds in new ways and extract new kinds of information from them. New techniques of analysis allow us to identify the place of origin of various materials, such as particular types of stone, which help us to interpret patterns of trade. Other analytical techniques allow us to assess technological achievements, such as the mastery of alloy metallurgy. Perhaps the most significant of all are the new independent dating techniques, by far the most important of which is radiocarbon (C14) dating. The establishment of an accurate chronology independent of historical dates (though I must emphasize that we are still some way from attaining this desirable objective) allows us to assess such factors as the duration of phases of development, the speed of change and the relationships between different areas; it can help us sort out what is cause and what effect and indeed provides the chronological perspective which is absolutely necessary for any kind of understanding of the growth and development of ancient civilization.

As important as the new discoveries of the last thirty years and the new techniques which have been developed during this time are the new attitudes that scholars have come to adopt. Until relatively recently archaeological writings have been dominated by the concept of peoples; major changes in the archaeological record have been explained in terms of movements of people and replacements of one people by another. Only recently has this preoccupation begun to be replaced by an interest in the process of cultural development and the causes and mechanisms of social change. The adoption of these ideas is very far from complete. Much of the literature about the early civilizations still attributes their growth to the innate genius of the Sumerians, the Egyptians and the Indus Valley population, without so much as a glance at the complex pattern of environmental, economic and social pressures acting on these societies. However, where the new approach has been adopted, especially in conjunction with some of the new techniques discussed above, it has begun to yield very interesting results. We are beginning to understand the patterns of population growth and clustering that preceded and accompanied the urban revolution. We are gaining insight into the nature of trade in western Asia in the period from about 8000 bc onwards, which was crucial to the emergence and survival of civilization, especially in Mesopotamia. We are learning, too, of the conditions under which economic specialization began to develop. None of these studies is, of course, totally new; indeed it is fair to say that all these matters were engaging Gordon Childe as long ago as the 1920s. However, it is only since we have freed ourselves from the obsession with population movements that dominated prehistoric studies in the early part of this century that we have made much progress in understanding the processes of cultural development.

The outlook for the future, as seen from 1976, is optimistic. A large part of the remains of the ancient civilizations is still to be excavated. And we know that we can tackle these excavations with a battery of more sensitive techniques than have been available in the past. Moreover another group of techniques enables us to undertake the analysis of the finds with more far-reaching results than ever before. And finally we are approaching the subject with a new range of questions directed at new objectives. I think that by the end of the present century we shall have achieved a very thorough understanding of the ancestry, the genesis and the development of the world's first cities.

Chapter III Mesopotamia : Land, Cities and People

The land

The earliest civilization in the world arose in the lands enclosed between the Tigris and Euphrates rivers, which we know by the Greek name Mesopotamia (meaning literally 'between the rivers'). In the second and first millennia BC this land between the rivers supported populous and wealthy cities from the highlands in the north to the Persian Gulf in the south, but the earliest flowering of civilization occurred in the much smaller area south of the capital of present-day Iraq, Baghdad. This region, of only about 26,000 square kilometres, was known to its first literate inhabitants as Shumer (perhaps the Shinar of the Bible) and we know their civilization as Sumerian. The main settlement was not in fact on the alluvial plain between the rivers but on the banks of the rivers themselves. All the main cities of Sumer were sited on the banks of the Tigris, the Euphrates or one of their tributaries; those that are today in open country were originally situated on the rivers, which are known to have changed course several times during the history of the area. Although the fertile soil of the alluvial plain grew the crops to support the expanding population of the cities, it was the rivers themselves that were the life-blood of Sumer and later Mesopotamian civilizations. In the first place, they provided water for consumption and irrigation, without which no society could exist in the arid climatic conditions of southern Mesopotamia. Secondly, they provided an easy means of communication and of transport of goods between the cities of the land. And, finally, they provided access to the Persian Gulf in the south and thereby to maritime contact and trade with countries bordering the Indian Ocean.

The country of Sumer was no land of milk and honey: the first inhabitants, who arrived in about 5000 bc, some two thousand years before the main flowering of Sumerian civilization, did not move into an earthly paradise. The land was indeed potentially rich in one of the most basic of

33

all natural resources—fertile soil—and by 5000 bc technology was sufficiently developed to exploit this potential, but the prosperous and thriving cities, that seemed to the Sumerian scribes to have existed from the beginning of time, were in reality created laboriously out of a land of contrasting arid plains and watery swamps, devoid of all mineral resources and vulnerable to disastrous flooding. Hydrologists believe that, at the time when the first settlers arrived in Sumer, the climate was very much as it is today: hot, arid and semi-tropical, with rain restricted to light falls in winter. One consequence of this for human settlement is clear: it would have been impossible to farm using only natural rainfall and the practice of cereal agriculture would have depended on irrigation. Indeed irrigation is a concept inseparably linked with Mesopotamia in popular thought and this is correct: the courses of old irrigation channels crisscrossing the Mesopotamian plain are visible everywhere and the ancient tablets are full of references to the construction and maintenance of dykes and canals. However, it would be a mistake to imagine that the massive irrigation works we know from the Babylonian period of the second millennium BC were necessary—or practicable—from the beginning. Quite modest measures, like the damming of existing streams, diverting small quantities of water into small channels, would have allowed the cultivation of considerable plots of land and would have been within the competence of small groups, even individual families, to organize.

If scholars are agreed that the climate has not changed significantly since the fifth millennium BC, there is no equivalent agreement about the coastline. Many authorities have thought that the coast of the Persian Gulf was considerably further north in Sumerian times. This view was derived originally from the ancient documents, which implied that cities like Eridu and Ur were close to the sea: a tablet of about 2000 BC specifically describes Eridu as lying on the sea coast. Moreover, support came from the apparently reasonable supposition that the large quantities of sediment which the Tigris and Euphrates bring down from the mountains, if deposited at the head of the Persian Gulf, would have caused the coastline to advance gradually southwards. However, recent studies have shown that the rivers have deposited all their sediment *before* they reach the sea and that therefore there is no reason to believe that the coastline was ever further north. Some geologists in fact believe that it may originally have been further *south*—and the absence of archaeological remains south of Eridu can be explained by the possibility that ancient sites are lying buried under great depths of silt. Archaeologists think this unlikely and certainly the Sumerian documents seem to refer to Eridu as the most southerly of their cities and indeed in their mythology the first to be created. Perhaps the most likely explanation is that the coastline was more or less where it is today, but that the marshy area interspersed with freshwater lakes at the head of the Gulf did not support large cities. This area today absorbs 90 per

34

Women found buried with other court retainers in the Royal Cemetery at Ur were lavishly adorned with jewellery. ▶

cent of the water of the Tigris and the Euphrates before they reach the Gulf; if this were the case in Sumerian times, this area of alternating marsh and open water might have been regarded as 'sea' by the Sumerians and the fact that the Euphrates was navigable would explain the references in the documents describing Ur and Eridu as ports.

The alluvial soils of southern Mesopotamia were very fertile and when irrigated produced much higher crop yields than the poorer soils of the plateaux or of the mountain valleys where farming had been first developed. This increasing production was almost certainly one of the necessary preconditions for the emergence of civilization in western Asia. However, unlike the farmers of the Nile valley where the different conditions of flooding and drainage preserved soil fertility indefinitely (or to be precise, until the construction of the Aswan dam in our own time), all Mesopotamian farmers had to contend with steadily declining conditions and decreasing crop yields. Their particular enemy was salt. Salt was spread over the surface of the land through the evaporation of slightly saline ground water and irrigation water, while the Mesopotamian rainfall was inadequate to wash it away. So the salt content of the soil, especially in the south, increased steadily. The Sumerians recognized the destructive effects of saline soil and combated them by limiting crops to one harvest per year (two were usual in the early period) and by growing crops which have a high tolerance of salt. The date palm has a particularly high tolerance, approaching 2 per cent of salt in the soil, while barley can tolerate nearly 1 per cent, wheat less than 0·5 per cent. A study by Thorkild Jacobsen of archives referring to the Diyala area showed that in about 2400 BC, wheat formed 16 per cent of the total cereal crop (composed of wheat and barley together); by 2100 BC wheat had dropped to about 2 per cent and after 2000 BC wheat does not appear in the records at all. Jacobsen indeed suggested that the decline of Sumerian civilization and the northward shift of political power in Babylonian times could be explained entirely as a result of the increasing salination of the soil. Initially, however, there would have been no problem, and in the south the food from cereal crops and date palms and from domesticated animals could have been supplemented by plentiful game—animals, birds and fish—from the marshes. When the first settlers arrived in southern Mesopotamia, they found a land with the potential for intensive and varied food-production.

There is one other point I must make here about the nature of the southern Mesopotamian countryside which, in a negative way, contributed vitally to the development of civilization. This is its total lack of the resources necessary for the support of civilized life, apart from the means of intensive production of food. The alluvial soils of southern Mesopotamia completely lacked all mineral resources, including those important to prehistoric man, such as building stone, siliceous rocks, metal ores or

◀ *Imported gold and lapis lazuli were worked into headdresses and necklaces for the women of the Mesopotamian court.*

37

precious stones. Indeed it lacked even adequate building timber, since the plain was treeless and the marsh vegetation did not include the trees which produce large, strong timbers. If the southern Mesopotamians wanted these materials, they *had* to obtain them from the mountain and plateau regions flanking the plain and, indeed, in the case of some commodities, from much further afield. This necessity was a keystone in the construction of Sumerian civilization.

The people

It is the most natural thing in the world when confronted by an ancient civilization to ask 'Who made it?', but to that question, put about the first Mesopotamian civilization, it is difficult to give an answer that is either sensible or helpful. Mesopotamian civilization was created by the inhabitants of southern Iraq of the fourth millennium BC. We call them the Sumerians, but this is simply a descriptive term taken from the name of the country as it appears on inscriptions in the title 'King of Sumer and Agade'. It is worth noting that they did not call themselves by this name: they described themselves as 'the black-headed people', which is no more helpful and rather less elegant than the descriptive terms used by modern scholars. The term Sumerian was applied first to the language identified on the earliest clay tablets and later to the whole civilization; we do not know whether it coincided with an ethnic grouping or not. As to the origin of the population that created this civilization, the language scholars and the archaeologists are in profound disagreement. This disagreement is unlikely to be resolved, unless one or other of the disciplines changes direction: in the present state of studies each uses assumptions that are unacceptable to the other. I shall outline the problem here.

The linguistic problem

Clay tablets from the first half of the third millennium BC have yielded evidence of three different languages. The main one is Sumerian itself, which is of the type known as *agglutinative*, which means that it is formed of roots which themselves do not change, but are modified by the addition of separate elements. Other languages of this sort include Turkish and the Finno-Ugrian group (as Oppert had so percipiently recognized in 1869), but Sumerian has no genetic affinity with any of them. The second main language to appear on the tablets is Akkadian; this, unlike Sumerian, is a Semitic tongue, related to modern Arabic and Hebrew. Semitic languages are not agglutinative, but *inflected*, which means that the roots themselves alter: in Semitic languages the root is usually composed of three consonants and differences of number, gender, tense etc. are shown by the insertion of different vowels between the consonants.

Babylon lies in ruins on a branch of the Euphrates. As in ancient Mesopotamian days, virtual desert flanks a narrow band of irrigated land by the river.

In the Early Dynastic period Akkadian appears mostly in the form of Semitic personal names in Sumerian texts, but there are a few tablets and inscriptions of this period actually written in the Semitic language, for instance the inscription on the base of a statue of Lugal-zagge-si at Nippur—a king of Uruk who reigned over all Sumer from about 2400 BC in the period immediately before the Empire of Sargon of Agade. Sargon was a Semitic speaker and the Akkadian language became the dominant tongue in his dynasty. Indeed, although there was a renaissance of Sumerian language and literature under the Third Dynasty of Ur (c. 2113–2096 BC) it was Akkadian that was written, and presumably spoken, all over Mesopotamia in the second millennium BC and was the language of international trade throughout the whole Near and Middle East. It is thought that the Sumerian and the Akkadian languages were initially spoken by different groups of people, with Sumerian dominant in the south and Akkadian from about Kish northwards. Whether this difference coincided with a *racial* distinction is unknown, although it is very often assumed to be the case. Anyway, by the second millennium BC the Akkadian language was in general use, whatever the racial origins of the people using it. The third language to appear on the tablets poses a different problem: it takes the form of a number of words thought to be of non-Sumerian and non-Semitic origin but incorporated into Sumerian. Language scholars deduce that these were taken over from a language spoken by a population that inhabited southern Mesopotamia before the arrival of speakers of Sumerian: they place particular weight on the fact that among the non-Sumerian words are a number of place-names (including their names for the Tigris and Euphrates). However, place-names are notoriously difficult to interpret and the linguistic evidence for the existence of a completely separate language seems flimsy. And, as we shall see, the archaeological evidence does not support the idea of a distinction between a pre-Sumerian population and the Sumerian population.

The archaeological evidence

The Mesopotamian plains were occupied rather late in prehistory, for the simple reason that the environment is unsuitable for the kinds of subsistence economy practised by man before about 6000 bc—hunting and gathering, or agriculture dependent on rainfall only. Thus, whereas both hunting and early farming sites (the latter belonging to the eighth and seventh millennia bc) occur on the flanks of the Zagros mountains, in the Levant and in southern Anatolia, the first Mesopotamian settlements on the northern plain belong to the early sixth millennium bc and their agriculture was already dependent on irrigation, while the southern plain may not have been settled before 5000 bc. The sequence of cultures worked out by archaeologists from excavations all over the country shows a marked divergence between the north and the south. The earliest phase in the north (named Hassuna-Samarra after two sites with different styles of painted pottery) was followed by the Halaf culture, which spread over a large part of northern Mesopotamia in the late sixth and fifth millennia and was characterized by prosperous, well-developed farming communities that were in all probability metal-using. Both the Hassuna-Samarra and the Halaf cultures had connections with Anatolia.

The story reconstructed from excavations in southern Mesopotamia is different: the earliest occupation yet recorded is no earlier than about 5000 bc and throughout the prehistoric period the connections were not with the north or the north-west, but rather with the east, with Khuzistan and highland Iran. Two early occupation phases which are not well known are named after the sites of Eridu and Hajji Muhammad respectively; they were followed by the Ubaid culture, the first well-known culture of the alluvial lowlands. In the mid-fifth millennium bc the Ubaid culture spread over the whole of Mesopotamia, bringing the Halaf culture to an apparently abrupt end. In addition it had trading connections over a much wider area, including parts of the Persian Gulf. The Ubaid population probably lived in towns of some size; they built monumental temples and had an already complex social and economic organization. The next phase of occupation in Mesopotamia is named after the site of Uruk and this was succeeded by the Jamdat Nasr phase, now more often known as the protoliterate period because it was succeeded immediately by the fully literate Early Dynastic phase of Sumerian history. Some authorities use neither of these terms, but call this phase late Uruk, since it clearly represents a late development of the Uruk culture.

It is not my purpose to discuss the prehistoric cultures of Mesopotamia, although I shall have to go into some aspects of their development when I discuss the origins of civilization. Here I am concerned only with the specific problem of the origin of Sumerian people. As we have seen, the linguistic evidence is sometimes used to support the idea that they were newcomers in southern Mesopotamia at a relatively late date (shortly before 3000 bc is frequently suggested). The archaeological evidence, on the other hand, speaks very strongly for continuity of settlement. There appears to be a direct development from the very earliest phase of occupation in southern Mesopotamia right through to the Early Dynastic period. Over this long period the only dramatic changes were in pottery styles: the picture revealed by archaeology is of steadily increasing prosperity and growing social complexity, but *no* abrupt change. Although, in the past, archaeologists have often taken changes in pottery style to indicate the arrival of a new people, this is rarely accepted today. In southern Mesopotamia the evidence for continuity is exceptionally strong. Take, for example, the city of Eridu, regarded by the Sumerians themselves as the oldest of their cities. Excavations have shown that the site was occupied from the very earliest phase of occupation known in southern Mesopotamia, which was indeed identified on this site and named after it. Particularly important is the excavation of a series of temples built one on top of the other in a sanctuary, which in its historical phase was dedicated to Enki, the god of water and wisdom and patron deity of Eridu. Under a ziggurat of about 2100 BC, one of the staged temple towers of Mesopotamia, the remains of no fewer than seventeen religious buildings were excavated. The earliest three were modest shrines of the Eridu and Hajji Muhammad phases, which gradually grew into spacious temples during the Ubaid and Uruk phases. Moreover, the floor of one of the early temples was covered by a thick layer of fish scales, suggesting strongly that the sanctuary was already dedicated to a water god. The inference is very strong that there was an unbroken religious tradition from the earliest settlement through the Early Dynastic period to late third millennium times. No other site has produced such impressive evidence of continuity as Eridu, but it is true that all Sumerian cities which have been excavated to sufficiently low levels prove to have been built on settlements of the Ubaid period. Eridu, Ur, Uruk and Lagash all had Ubaid foundations, as did several sites in northern Mesopotamia. If the evidence for continuity between the Ubaid and Uruk periods is still not accepted by everyone (and those who believe in an influx of population from outside usually suggest it coincides with the beginning of the Uruk period), the evidence of continuity from the Uruk period into Early Dynastic times is very strong indeed. As well as evidence of continuity in the use and building of temples on many sites, there is the evidence of the writing. We know that the tablets of the Early Dynastic period, inscribed in the cuneiform script, are written in Sumerian. And it seems that the writing we find on these Early Dynastic tablets evolved directly out of the pictographic writing of the earliest tablets of all, which belong to the Uruk period (a stone tablet from early Uruk levels at Kish and a collection of 500–600 clay tablets from late Uruk levels at Uruk itself). These early tablets mostly comprise straightforward lists of objects and quantities and, as the objects are represented simply by pictures (clearly recognizable although already stylized), it is possible to 'read' these tablets without knowing what language they record. However, with the help of the tablets from the succeeding Jamdat Nasr (protoliterate) phase, we can trace the evolution of many of the original pictograms into the cuneiform signs of the Early Dynastic period. This suggests strongly that the earliest tablets already recorded the Sumerian language.

Thus we have strong evidence of continuity from the Uruk period into Early Dynastic times and a considerable probability of continuity from the earliest phase of settlement. To the archaeologist it seems likely that Sumerian civilization was created by the descendants of the people who first occupied southern Mesopotamia around 5000 bc.

Outline of Sumerian history

The writing of Mesopotamian history is extremely difficult, especially in its early phases. The Mesopotamians did not chronicle their own history. The earliest records we have are tablets giving temple accounts, and indeed more than 90 per cent of all Sumerian tablets are economic, legal and administrative documents. The remaining 10 per cent comprise literary and religious texts, educational 'school-books' and a few scientific works, from some of which it is possible to extract information about political and military history. However, the record extracted from the tablets can be confirmed and expanded by the evidence of inscriptions on monuments which fortunately give the name of the king who built it and his city of origin.

The most useful of all documents is the Sumerian King List which I have already discussed in connection with chronology. This, however, begins in pure fable (with reigns of many thousands of years attributed to the eight or ten kings before the Flood) and ends as an apparently reliable record. The problem for the historian is to estimate which information he can accept from the middle part of the list. Actually it seems that even the earliest part referring to kings who reigned *after* the Flood, though clearly still legendary in the sense that individual kings are awarded reigns of a thousand years or more, preserves the names of actual rulers. For instance, the name of En-me-barage-si, twenty-second king of the First Dynasty of Kish (first to rule after the Flood according to the King List) has been found on an inscription, as has Mes-anne-padda, founder of the First Dynasty of Ur. It is probable also that the four famous rulers of Uruk who figure in the Sumerian epic tales—Enmerkar, Lugulbanda, Dumuzi and Gilgamesh—really existed.

Even if the Sumerian King List contains more fact than fiction, like the Homeric poems of Greece, it is still difficult to use as a historical record. The picture that emerges for the whole of the Early Dynastic period is one of more or less independent and often warring city states; at most times one city was recognized as supreme, but this supremacy shifted from city to city. The King List, which records only kings who reigned over the whole of Sumer, records Kish, Uruk, Ur and Lagash as supreme at different stages of the Early Dynastic period. There is evidence also of intrusions from outside: at one stage dynasties from Elam (south-west Iran) ruled over at least part of Sumer and at a later date kings of Mari (far to the north-west on the upper Euphrates) dominated the country. At the very end of the Early Dynastic period a king of Umma, Lugal-zagge-si, captured Lagash and then proceeded to capture the rest of Sumer; indeed he may have held sway over a much larger area, if his own boastful inscriptions are to be believed. In any case his empire, if that is what it was, ended with his reign (*c.* 2400–2371 BC), when the Semitic king, Sargon of Agade (Akkad) came—bloodily—to power. The beginning of

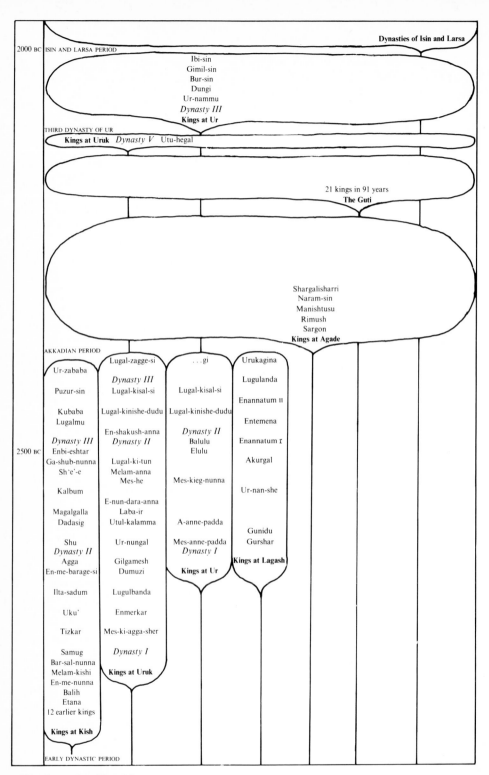

The Sumerian King List.

this 'Semitic episode' is taken to mark the end of the Early Dynastic period.

Alongside this historical account of the Early Dynastic period, we have an archaeological account, which is based on archaeological criteria such as the changing styles of pottery and other artefacts. An archaeologist excavating a site in Sumer is frequently unable to assign any building or deposit to the reign of a king who figures in the King List or even, in many cases, to a dynasty. He is, however, perfectly able to assign it to an archaeological phase, which has a clear *relative* position in the archaeological sequence, though it may have no absolute dates attached to it. In fact archaeologists divide the Early Dynastic period into three phases. The latest of these, Early Dynastic III, ends at a known date with the advent of Sargon of Agade in about 2370 BC. For convenience I shall allow an arbitrary 200 years or so for each of the three Early Dynastic phases: E.D.I 3000–2800 BC; E.D.II 2800–2600 BC and E.D.III 2600–2370 BC, but these are no more than guesses at the moment. If we attempt to correlate these phases with the historical account derived from the King List, we can make an approximate equation between E.D.III and the period of the First and Second Dynasties of Ur (for which the King List allots a period of a little more than 250 years before the rise of Sargon), while the E.D.I and II periods can be correlated with the First Dynasty of Kish, for which, however, the King List provides us with only 'legendary' reigns of many hundreds of years. Even this approximate correlation gives rise to problems. The main one stems from the discovery of the Royal Tombs of Ur. The material from these tombs belongs to the E.D.III period in style and the three radiocarbon dates we have give a mean corrected date of about 2500 BC which fits the dates suggested on historical grounds for the E.D.III period. However, the kings buried in these tombs, Mes-kalam-dug and A-kalam-dug (as we know from their seals and other inscriptions) do not appear in the King List at all. It has been suggested therefore that they belong to a time before the First Dynasty of Ur, before kings of Ur ruled over the whole of Sumer. On the historical chronology this would make them predate about 2650 BC, which, however, seems too early for E.D.III and for the radiocarbon dates. No satisfactory solution to this problem has yet been suggested.

With the end of the Early Dynastic period and the beginning of the Sargonid era we are on much firmer historical ground. The Sargonid or Akkadian period lasted less than 150 years, but it altered the course of Mesopotamian history. The two great kings of this dynasty, of which there were only five altogether, were its founder Sargon (2371–2316 BC) and his grandson Naram-sin (2291–2255 BC), who was fourth in the succession. These two rulers, who were based on the still undiscovered site of Agade, not only subdued all the Sumerian city states, but they conquered northern Mesopotamia and Elam as well, to establish the first

Mesopotamian empire. They described themselves as kings of the 'Four Quarters of the World' and, in Mesopotamian terms, it was no idle boast. However, they were under constant attack both from revolts within the empire and from incursions of nomadic peoples on the fringes. It was one of these, the Guti, hailing from the northern Zagros mountains, which finally brought down the Sargonid empire shortly before 2200 BC. The Sargonid period saw great political, social, economic and cultural changes and many of the innovations of this time remained permanent attributes of Mesopotamian society.

About the Guti, who overthrew the Sargonid empire, we know very little. They appear to coincide with a period of anarchy: the Sumerian King List asks rather plaintively 'Who was king? Who was not king?' It records in all 21 kings with a combined reign of 91 years. The last of the line was defeated in about 2120 BC by a king of Uruk called Utu-hegal. However, after a reign of only seven years, Utu-hegal was overthrown by one of his own officials, Ur-nammu, governor of Ur, who took the titles 'King of Ur, King of Sumer and Agade'. The dynasty which he founded, the Third Dynasty of Ur, lasted for just over a century (c. 2113–2000 BC). This was a period of Sumerian renaissance and appears as one of the most creative and brilliant episodes of Mesopotamian history. This was the period in which the most famous and impressive *ziggurats*, best known of all Mesopotamian monuments, were built and it is also the period which produced much of the Sumerian literature we have (though it is largely known from later copies). The earliest law code yet found also belongs to this time, preceding that of Hammurabi by three centuries or more.

The Third Dynasty of Ur collapsed in the years before 2000 BC as a result of incursions both of Elamites from the east and, more importantly, of Amorites from the west. For about two centuries after this Mesopotamia existed as a mosaic of kingdoms of differing sizes, the most important being Isin and Larsa in the south, Assur and Eshnunna in the north. During the Dynasties of Isin and Larsa the political centre of gravity shifted slowly but irresistibly northwards till it settled finally in Babylon. With the defeat of Rim-sin, the last king of the Larsa Dynasty, by Hammurabi in the eighteenth century BC, Babylon won control of the whole country and Sumer disappeared in a Babylonian kingdom. We shall not follow Mesopotamian history beyond this point, since our concern is with the early stages, but I must mention here the fact that we owe much of our knowledge of the Sumerians to the Old Babylonian kingdom. During this period was founded what is known as the Old Babylonian literary tradition, which incorporated many Sumerian traditions in a form that enabled them to survive the later Dark Age and be revived by Neo-Babylonian and Neo-Assyrian scribes in the first millennium BC.

City states and cities in the Early Dynastic period

Our knowledge of the Early Dynastic period is derived from both documentary and archaeological sources. The documents tell us a lot about Sumerian society, about the economic and social organization, about the practices and beliefs of the Sumerians, about their theoretical knowledge and to some extent about their history. Moreover, they allow us that privilege denied to prehistorians—a glimpse into the very minds and hearts of men. But they leave us strangely in ignorance of the physical, tangible environment of the Sumerians: they do not describe their cities, their houses or their land; nor do they describe their belongings, the familiar everyday objects that make up the individual's immediate environment, and they do not, with a very few exceptions, describe daily life. Of course to the Sumerians such descriptions would have seemed pointless: these were things that everyone knew. But to us the effect of the lack is frustrating and also rather curious. From the documents we get a picture of a rather rarified culture of the mind—a world of gods and heroes, of great works and superhuman emotions—balanced, it is true, by an enormous number of administrative documents, but not by accounts of everyday activities. It is as though we are dealing with a world of gods and kings on the one hand and civil servants on the other, but are somehow missing out on ordinary people. Fortunately it is these very gaps in the documentary evidence that archaeology is best equipped to fill and using both sources we can build up a fairly well rounded picture of Sumerian civilization.

The documentary sources for the Early Dynastic period refer exclusively to Sumer proper, that is to Mesopotamia south of about Baghdad. However, archaeological excavations have shown us that important towns existed in other parts of Mesopotamia and these had a strongly Sumerian aspect: far-flung examples are Assur on the Tigris, about 250 kilometres north of Baghdad as the crow flies, Tell Taya, about 100 kilometres further north still and, in the north-west, Mari on the Euphrates, about 350 kilometres from Baghdad. Much closer to the modern capital, but still outside Sumer proper, are Khafaje (ancient Tutub) and Tell Asmar (ancient Eshnunna) in the Diyala area, which were to all intents and purposes Sumerian cities. The recently excavated site of Tell Taya, is of great importance because it employed stone as building material instead of the usual mud-brick and has yielded the only reasonably complete Mesopotamian town plan of the Early Dynastic period that we have. These northern sites have produced much of our most useful archaeological information and we know from a few fragmentary finds that they were not entirely without writing, but about these cities the documents from the southern centres are silent. While a pan-Mesopotamian urban culture was already in existence before 2500 BC, the political and cultural centre, where civilization crystallized and political power was concentrated, was in Sumer itself and for much of the time in the extreme south of Sumer:

of the four cities which according to the King List produced major dynasties that ruled Sumer between the Flood and the Agade period, only Kish is more than 80 kilometres from the marshland which probably formed the southern border of the country in Sumerian times.

During the Early Dynastic period there were probably never more than twenty city states in Sumer and possibly fewer. The fourteen most important cities were, from south to north: Eridu, Ur, Larsa, Uruk, Bad-tibira, Lagash, Umma, Shuruppak, Adab, Nippur, Larak, Akshak, Kish and Sippar. Each city state consisted of a walled city with suburbs and satellite towns and villages contained in a territory which included gardens, orchards, palm-groves and fields as well as areas of unirrigated steppe used for pasture. We do not know the area covered by any city state (perhaps several thousand square kilometres), but we know the size of some of the cities themselves: Ur enclosed about 60 hectares within its walls, while the largest of all Sumerian cities, Uruk, covered about 450 hectares—a size which no European city attained before the Roman Imperial period. Several estimates of population size have been made, but they suffer from the disadvantages that we do not know whether densities derived from modern analogies have any validity and in any case we do not know how much of a Sumerian city was occupied by dwellings, nor what proportion of the total population lived outside the city in suburbs, villages or small towns. Many of the estimates are probably too high. We should perhaps not be far wrong if we thought in terms of populations of 10,000–20,000 for most of the cities, with perhaps 50,000 at Uruk; if we were to allow half as much again for the rural population, we should arrive at a total population for the whole of Early Dynastic Sumer of several hundred thousand. The round figure of half a million has been suggested, giving a population density over the whole area of approximately 20 people per square kilometre.

What were Sumerian cities like? What would our reactions be if we could be transported by some convenient 'Time Machine' into early third-millennium Uruk or Ur or Lagash? As we approached our Sumerian city on such an imaginary journey, our first impression, from the outside, would probably be of the massive city wall. The earliest wall at Uruk, supposedly the work of the hero Gilgamesh himself, had a circumference of about 9·5 kilometres; it consisted of a double rampart, the inner one of which had a core 4–5 metres thick built of the plano-convex bricks which characterize Early Dynastic buildings (flat on one face but rounded on the other so that the courses had to be laid not flat but in herring-bone fashion). There were semicircular towers at regular intervals and rectangular ones flanking the entrances. This wall was a source of pride to the Sumerians themselves. A late version of the Gilgamesh epic exhorts the reader to 'look at it still today: the outer wall where the cornice runs, it shines with the brilliance of copper; and the inner wall, it has no equal. . . . Climb

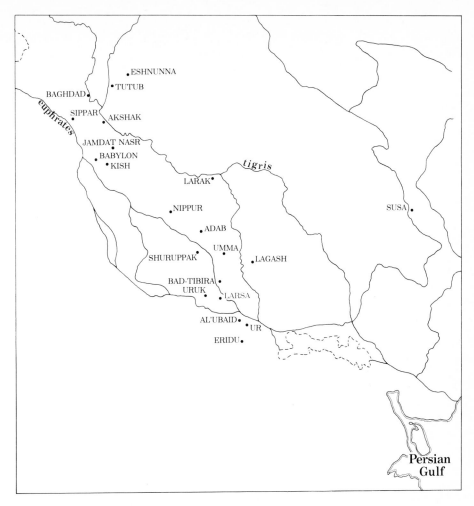

The most important cities in Sumer before about 2500 BC (Mesopotamia south of modern Baghdad) were Eridu, Ur, Larsa, Uruk, Bad-Tibira, Lagash, Umma, Shuruppak, Adab, Nippur, Larak, Kish, Akshak and Sippar. Tutub and Eshnunna lay outside Sumer but were to all intents and purposes Sumerian. Susa was centre of a parallel development. Al'Ubaid and Jamdat Nasr were settlements dating from before the rise of the cities, Babylon a later capital.

upon the wall of Uruk; walk along it, I say; regard the foundation terrace and examine the building; is it not burnt brick and good?'

   After the impressive dimensions of the defences, our attention would be taken, I think, by the building material. As we have noted, southern Mesopotamia lacks entirely both good building timber and stone and thus, with very few exceptions, all buildings were made of sun-dried bricks of mud. To western eyes this is at first sight strange, but it is a cheap and easily obtained building material, suitable for a climate with little rainfall

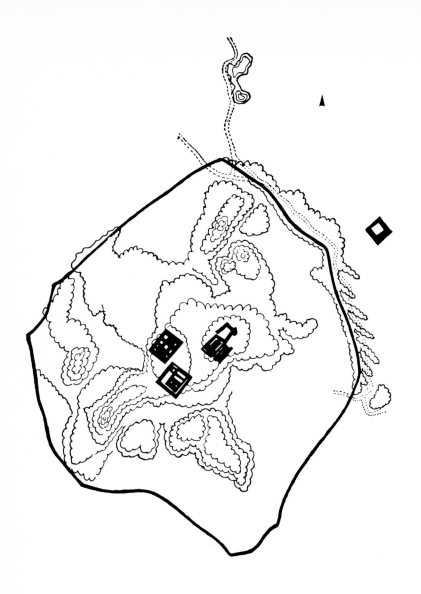

Ur's walls (left) enclosed 60 hectares. Uruk, perhaps originally comprising two communities, was an exceptional 450 hectares in area (above).

By about 1900 BC Ur (right) was a web of streets and, like other Sumerian cities, can never have been laid out to a plan. A wealthy house of this period (below) had an open court-yard in place of a central room.

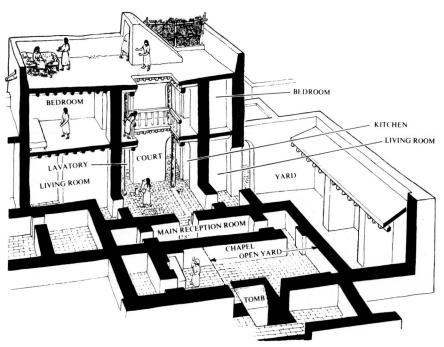

Mud-bricks (below) were the normal building material in Mesopotamia. Sun-baked and bonded with liquid mud, they were quickly assembled and easily repaired. In rare cases, as at Tell Taya in the far north (above), stone was used.

and it is still characteristic of rural, and to some extent urban, buildings over much of the Near and Middle East today.

Once inside the gates we should probably find ourselves in a densely built up maze of buildings, sometimes laid out on a regular grid of narrow streets, more often on an unplanned collection of winding alleys. In the central area were the main public buildings of the cities—the temples, massive buildings set in enclosures separated actually and symbolically from the rest of the town by surrounding walls. Multi-coloured decoration that was usually made of clay cone mosaic frequently adorned the temple walls. This use of colour, together with the great size of the temples and their position on a raised platform (sometimes on a true *ziggurat*), would instantly have set them apart from the modest dun-coloured mud-brick buildings of the rest of the town. Also occupying a central position would have been the royal palace enclosure, which certainly by the end of the Early Dynastic period would have rivalled the temple in size and splendour.

From these central buildings the streets radiated out towards the gates. The houses of the well-off lay along the main streets, with humbler dwellings between and behind them. Though a few of the wealthier buildings had two storeys, most Sumerian houses were single-storeyed, flat-roofed buildings, consisting of subsidiary rooms clustered around one larger central room: only in the Sargonid period did it become customary to arrange the rooms round a central courtyard. The main streets were wide enough to accommodate a wheeled vehicle, the alleys very narrow and tortuous. All the streets were unpaved, but there was at least a rudimentary system of sewage conduits beneath them. There may have been open areas within the city walls, where we might encounter animals grazing.

So far, I think, we should have found ourselves reasonably at home in a Sumerian city, particularly if we were already familiar with Middle Eastern towns today, but as we wandered around we should begin to notice the absence of many of the features of urban life as we now know it. Apart from the temples and the palaces, there would be no public buildings: no houses of parliament, no law-courts, no libraries, no hospitals or schools, no theatres or opera-houses. Still more noticeable would be the complete absence of shops or market place; absent too would be factories and workshops. In fact many of the activities that take place in buildings of these types in European cities did exist in Sumer, but during the Early Dynastic period they flourished under the auspices of the temple and palace households. From the Sargonid period onward we do find some of these other public buildings separately in the cities, but in Early Dynastic times it is within the temple and palace compounds that we must look for store-houses, workshops, libraries and perhaps schools. What was lacking in Sumerian civilization of the Early Dynastic period, or at least in the early part of it, that seems so fundamental to Western urbanism today and indeed to European urbanism from the archaic Greeks onwards (but not to the civilization of the Minoans and Mycenaeans) was private enterprise. The degree to which this did exist is much disputed, but I adhere to what is now a rather old-fashioned view that the Sumerian economy in its early phases was a form of state ownership, though not one of the forms familiar to us in the twentieth century AD. We might describe it as 'God ownership' (sometimes called theocratic socialism): the city was conceived to be not only ruled but *owned* by a god, which served as a symbol of collective identity for the citizens of that town. For instance, Eridu belonged to Enki, the sea-god; Ur to Nanna, the moon-god; Lagash to Ningursu; Nippur to Enlil, the air-god and Uruk to two gods: Anu, the sky-god and Inanna, the goddess of love. Land was actually owned by the god and administered for him by the temple community, which organized the production, concentration and re-distribution of food and supported specialist officials, craftsmen and merchants.

In recent years this view of the nature of the Sumerian city state economy has been challenged, notably by the Russian scholar Diakanoff, working mainly on the temple documents from Lagash. He suggests that although the temple clearly owned a considerable fraction of the territory of the city state (perhaps something like one quarter) the rest of the land consisted of large estates owned by the king and the nobility and small plots of land owned by commoners. Certainly there exist documents from Shuruppak, Adab and Lagash of about 2500–2400 BC recording sales of property by private individuals. Clearly some private enterprise existed by this stage and many scholars, including Kramer, accept the Diakanoff view that in Sumerian society land was predominantly privately owned. However, it seems to me that to characterize Sumerian society in this manner, without considering its chronological development over the many centuries of its history, is dangerous. Even if Diakanoff's account is an accurate description of the Sumerian economy in 2400 BC, it does not follow that the situation was the same in 2800 BC, let alone 3200 BC. The fact is that we have large numbers of economic documents only from about 2500 BC onwards and for the earlier period we must depend largely on the archaeological evidence. If we use the documentary evidence from the later period, I suggest we should use it to project trends backwards, rather than to assume an unchanging position. We know that the role of private enterprise increased in importance during the period for which we *do* have documents. It seems logical, when attempting to reconstruct the economy of earlier periods, to put this trend into reverse and to project it backwards. If we do so we reach the conclusion that private enterprise was less important in the earliest phases of Mesopotamian civilization. This view is in accordance with archaeological evidence which indicates that before the Early Dynastic II period the temple was the only institution: before that time there is no evidence for the existence of the royal household or of an aristocracy. In the later periods the king and the noblemen were the chief landowners after the temple; the area held by commoners can never have been large. It seems likely that, before there were kings and noblemen, all, or almost all, the land belonged to the temple.

The American scholar Otto Edzard has made the interesting suggestion that there was a difference in the matter of private ownership between the northern cities, where the Akkadian language was dominant, and the ancient Sumerian cities of the south. Most of the documents relating to the private sale of land in the Early Dynastic period come from the north, while such documents are rare in the south before the second millennium BC. Thus the increase in private ownership may have been one of the contributions made by the Semitic speaking peoples to the development of Mesopotamian civilization. Edzard concludes, as did an earlier generation of scholars, that in the traditional Sumerian city state the temple was the chief owner of the land and I think he is right.

But now I shall return for a moment to our tour of a Sumerian city to see whether perhaps, with a further effort of the imagination, we can call up some shadowy figures with which to people it. Here the documents, which are so silent about the physical aspect of Sumerian cities, can help us more than the archaeological evidence. We know that most of the population of a Sumerian city was engaged in the production of food. Most of the people we passed in the streets would be farmers, market-gardeners, herdsmen or fishermen and correspondingly many of the goods being transported in carts (pulled by oxen or asses) or on pack animals (asses) or by hand would have been food products. However, some of the farmers would have other roles as well: carpenters, smiths, potters, stone-cutters, basket-makers, leather-workers, wool-spinners, bakers and brewers are all recorded, as are merchants and what we might call the 'civil service' of the temple community—the priests and the scribes. How many of these would have been full-time specialists we do not know. Robert Adams suggests that by the beginning of Early Dynastic times no more than about 20 per cent of the labour force was employed substantially on economic activities outside subsistence pursuits. Henri Frankfort indeed maintained that everyone was first and foremost a practical farmer and at 'seed time and harvest time every able-bodied man was no doubt on the land'. There is no simple answer to this question, particularly as it changed through time: by the end of the Early Dynastic period the quantity of trade and the development of manufacturing industry emerging from the archaeological and documentary records suggests that there must have been a considerable number of full-time specialists.

We have been talking so far about occupations, but what about social status? To what degree was this a class society and how apparent would class differences have been to us as we wandered around the city? This is another question to which there is no simple answer. We know that by the time of Hammurabi in the eighteenth century BC there was a formal division into three classes: noblemen, commoners and slaves. What we do not know is how far back in time this division went. The documents of the Early Dynastic period suggest differences in status and wealth but no rigid division into classes. We know that in principle all members of the temple community, except slaves, were equal: they were all equally servants of the god and equally devoted to his service; there was no leisured class. However, we also know that the allotments of land and the rations distributed by the temple organization were not all equal, though we do not know on what basis distinctions were made. We know too that the accumulation of private wealth was possible; Frankfort has written of a 'fringe of private enterprise' round the hard core of the temple economy. High social status was attached to certain occupations: priests, temple administrators and scribes, for instance, were clearly respected members of the community and they seem also to have been among the wealthiest of the citizens (excluding royalty). The palace with the king, the palace retinue and the military establishment (closely linked with the king in Sumer) provided another social elite, which grew in importance in the course of the Early Dynastic period. Indeed the increasing power of the king seems to have been closely associated with the crystallization of class stratification. At the bottom of the social ladder were slaves: to begin with these were few in number and were derived from foreign conquests, though later it was possible for a man to sell his children into slavery for money. Slaves were rarely privately owned, but formed a substantial part of the temple labour force: one temple archive suggests that 250 or 300 of the total force of about 1,200 were slaves. What about women in Sumerian society? Clearly their role in public life was minimal, though it was apparently possible for the role of the *en*, the chief priest of the temple, to be filled by a woman. We know of no female rulers (though the consorts of kings lived and died in appropriately sumptuous style), no female administrators or scribes, and, indeed, women received no education. Minor priestesses there were, as well as the occasional female *en*, but the major role of a priestess was to act the part of the goddess in the Sacred Marriage ceremony. Women's names sometimes appear in temple archives as holders of allotments, which indicates that they must have served the community directly in some way. At a different level, women served as temple prostitutes and slave girls were used in large numbers in the preparation of wool and in the temple kitchens and breweries. The roles of women as wives and mothers were similar to those of European societies. Interestingly, their rights and obligations were defined in law.

The people of Sumer wore woollen clothes—the men a flounced skirt (top right) and sometimes a felt cloak, the women a shawl-like garment draped over one shoulder (above). The women's hair was usually plaited on their heads.

To return once more to our tour of a Sumerian city, can we put features to the ghosts who stalk the streets? Can we clothe them? Can we give them tongue? The answer to all these questions is, up to a point, yes. From their skeletons we know that the Sumerians were of the long-headed 'Mediterranean' physical type; their statues show them as having big fleshy noses, enormous eyes and thick necks, but these traits may represent an artistic convention rather than realistic portraiture. The Sumerians described themselves as the 'black-headed people', a phrase which presumably describes hair colour rather than skin hue. Sumerian men were either clean shaven or wore a long beard; their hair was often long and parted in the middle, while women usually plaited their hair into a long braid which they wore wound round the head. The characteristic male dress in Early Dynastic times was a flounced woollen skirt and a felt cloak; women wore a long shawl-like garment covering the whole body except for the right shoulder which was left exposed. As to what they spoke, we have already seen that Sumerian was dominant in the south, the Semitic Akkadian language in the north: in our tour of Ur or Uruk or Lagash we should hear mostly Sumerian, though here and there we might catch a few Semitic words, especially names. If it were a northern Mesopotamian city we were visiting, however, we should probably hear exclusively Akkadian and even as far south as Kish we might find we were listening mostly to the Semitic tongue. Although there is a clear geographical division between the use of the two languages, there is no evidence that this coincided with any racial difference. Statues from Mari in the exclusively Semitic region far to the north-west, inscribed with indisputably Semitic names, show exactly the same physical type as those from southernmost Sumer, though, as I have mentioned, this may simply represent an artistic convention.

We have now finished our imaginary tour of a city of the early third millennium BC and I think the device has helped to give us some idea of what Sumerian cities were like. Now we shall go on to examine, both on the ground and in the literature, what A. Leo Oppenheim has called the 'Great Organizations'—the temple and the palace—the twin pillars of Sumerian city life.

Chapter IV Mesopotamia: Temple and Palace

The temple

It is impossible to overemphasize the importance of the institution of the temple in Mesopotamian society: it was in the first place the economic centre of the city (later the palace played a parallel role, but it never replaced the temple: the two functioned side by side). Indeed, as I shall explain later, it was probably through the mechanism of the temple economy that the Urban Revolution was accomplished in Mesopotamia. The antiquity of the temple as a building (and by implication as an institution also) we have already seen: simple shrines are found in the earliest occupation levels we have in southern Mesopotamia and by the Ubaid stage several full-scale temples are known. At Eridu we have a sequence of eighteen religious buildings one on top of the other, from a pre-Ubaid shrine at the base to a massive ziggurat temple of the end of the second millennium BC on the surface. Many Sumerian temples have been excavated and we have a good understanding of how they developed architecturally; our knowledge of how they were used is, on the other hand, decidedly sketchy. Here I shall not go into architectural history, but in order to convey some idea of the physical impact of these buildings I shall describe in detail a number of temples from different phases of Mesopotamian history.

The first in fact belongs to pure prehistory, before the time of any written record: it is the temple of the Ubaid period at Eridu, which was in all probability dedicated to Enki, the patron deity of Eridu, to whom the latest temple on the site undoubtedly belonged. The 'Ubaid period temple' was in fact no fewer than eight superimposed temples (numbers VI–XIII, numbered from the top downwards as they were excavated), overlying four pre-Ubaid shrines. Even the earliest temple of the Ubaid phase was already built on a substantial platform and its external wall had rectangular buttresses at regular intervals. By the latest phase (VI) the platform measured approximately 26·5 × 16 metres and the temple itself approximately 23·5 × 12·5 metres. The last three Ubaid period temples at Eridu (VIII–VI) had already acquired the tripartite form that became the standard plan of the Sumerian temple, its long central room (the 'nave'), with an altar at one end and an offering table at the other, flanked by symmetrically grouped side chambers (in two 'aisles'). This arrangement of the three areas was to become a feature of Near Eastern cult buildings of several different religions and is most familiar to us in the basic plan of the Christian church.

The largest of all the Sumerian cities, Uruk, boasted two major temple precincts: one, the Eanna sanctuary, was devoted to Inanna, the goddess of love; the other was dedicated to Anu, the sky-god. Both had a series of temples, the earliest of which were built in the Uruk period. The earliest preserved temple in the Eanna sanctuary is known as the Limestone Temple, because the lower parts of the walls, at least, were built of limestone blocks—a remarkable fact when we remember that there was no building stone available on the Mesopotamian plain. It occupied an area of about 76 × 30 metres and consisted of a central 'nave' with walls decorated with niches (a characteristic feature of Mesopotamian temple architecture) and symmetrically arranged side chambers of which one on each side had stairs leading to the flat roof. The most important room of the building, on the south, short side, was entered from the nave; it was flanked by two annexe rooms. While the plan and the niche decoration are typical traits, the use of limestone is exceptional, though not absolutely so (the platform of Temple III at Eridu was in fact faced with limestone blocks).

In the succeeding phase, the Limestone Temple was replaced by an even more impressive building, known as the Pillar Temple. This building, which has not been fully excavated, stood on a mud-brick platform and was approached through a portico or colonnade composed of a double row of four huge free-standing pillars (each 2·6 metres in diameter). These pillars, together with the walls of the adjacent court, which were made in the form of a series of half columns, and the platform were all decorated in the clay cone mosaic style characteristic of Sumerian temple architecture: patterns were made up of the painted bases of baked clay cones set into the mud plaster of the walls and always employed the colours red, black and white. They appear to copy textile patterns. While clay cones occur commonly, there is another temple (also in Uruk, situated between the two main sanctuaries of Anu and Inanna) in which *stone* cones were used: red and black limestone and white alabaster.

The massive temples of the Eanna sanctuary—the Limestone and Pillar Temples and their successors—represent a new development in temple architecture in Uruk times. By contrast the series of at least seven superimposed small temples excavated in the Anu sanctuary in the same

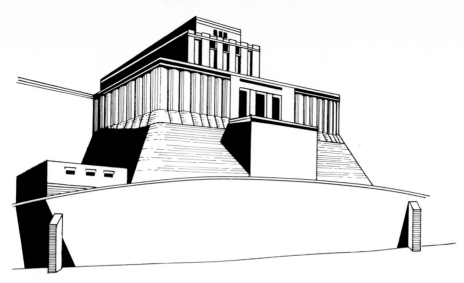

One of the earliest in a series of temples built successively on the one site at Eridu.

city preserve the tradition of the Ubaid period temples at Eridu. Each stood on an elevated platform which was raised with each successive re-construction until the final temple was perched on a veritable artificial mountain, a *ziggurat*. By the latest phase in this sanctuary the *ziggurat* had reached a height of about 13 metres; it was z-shaped in plan, measuring about 70×60 metres and had inward-sloping walls further strengthened by buttresses. The *ziggurat* or staged temple tower was to become the most characteristic feature of Mesopotamian temple architecture from the late third millennium BC onwards, but it had its origins in the relatively modest platforms of predynastic temples such as that we have been describing in the Anu precinct at Uruk. The best-preserved temple of this series is the latest and belongs to the late Uruk or Jamdat Nasr phase. It is known as the White Temple because of its whitewashed walls: measuring only about $22 \times 17 \cdot 5$ metres, it had the usual tripartite plan with 'nave' and 'aisles'; the whitewashed walls were decorated with elaborate buttresses and recesses.

For the Early Dynastic period I shall describe a small shrine on the site of al'Ubaid rather than one of the major city temples. It lies four miles west of Ur and overlies the settlement which has given this site's name to the major prehistoric period of southern Mesopotamia. Though unimpressive in size, this temple was exceptionally lavishly decorated. We are fortunate in having an inscription that tells us it was dedicated to Ninhursag, the Sumerian mother-goddess, and was built by A-anne-padda, son of Mes-anne-padda, who, according to the King List, founded the First Dynasty of Ur. We can therefore date the construction of the temple to before 2500 BC. This temple was the earliest of three. They were erected on a platform which had a superstructure of mud-brick built—unusually—

61

on stone foundations. Of the building itself little survived since it had been deliberately and violently destroyed, but the elaborate decorations, which were pitched over the edge of the platform, fortunately lay protected by debris from the later temples. From the positions in which they were found it was possible to work out where many of them probably originally belonged. The temple seems to have been a small rectangular building, of which only the main façade (the south-west wall) was decorated. From above the lintel of the main entrance probably came a large panel measuring about 2·3 × 1·05 metres. It is decorated in high relief with a scene of a lion-headed eagle (identified as the divine bird, Im-dugud) flanked by two stags. The panel itself was made of wood, covered by a layer of bitumen in which the finer detail of the relief was made up, and the whole was covered by thin hammered copper sheets: the effect is of a solid copper structure. The same technique was used to produce several small statuettes of bulls, which probably stood somewhere outside the temple on the platform, and six lions' heads, four large and two small, which came from somewhere near the entrance. Made in the same way too was a narrow frieze of copper-covered reliefs of young bulls and cows; this seems to have been attached to the façade wall some distance above ground level. Above this ran another frieze, made in a different manner, of shell and limestone figures inlayed in bitumen which provided a black background to the scenes depicted: a procession of bulls and a rather elaborate dairy scene showing the milking of cows and the making of butter (appropriate to the mother-goddess Ninhursag: a common claim made by early rulers was 'fed with the holy milk of Ninhursag'). Above this frieze there may have been a third, consisting only of identical limestone figures of birds on a bitumen background. Additional decorative features which probably flanked the entrance are a number of columns of two different kinds: both are made of palm logs covered with bitumen; one kind is covered with copper sheeting like the statues and the reliefs, while the other is covered with countless little triangular and lozenge-shaped pieces of red sandstone, mother of pearl and black shale, producing the red, white and black effect beloved of Mesopotamian temple architects and so often produced in the clay cone mosaic style. The same colour scheme is repeated at al'Ubaid, also in a version of the clay cone mosaic theme: in this case the heads of the clay pegs were shaped like saucers with wavy edges; in the centre of the saucer was a rounded piece of red sandstone, surrounded by red, white and black clay petals, set in bitumen. These were presumably wall decorations too, though we do not know precisely where they came from. But I think enough has been said to indicate the amount of labour and artistry that went into creating a thing of splendour out of what was, after all, only a small suburban shrine.

The last temple I am going to describe is probably the most impressive in the whole of Mesopotamia: the ziggurat built at Ur by Ur-

Mosaics of clay cones were a regular feature among elaborate decorations in the Mesopotamian temples, as in the Pillar Temple at Uruk (below). At al'Ubaid the cones had flower-like heads (as right) and a great bird, covered in sheet copper, hovered over the entrance (above).

nammu, founder of the Third Dynasty of Ur (2113–2096 BC) for the moon god, Nanna, over an earlier ziggurat of the Early Dynastic period. Ur-nammu's reign was a period of immense building activity: in all the major cities of Mesopotamia, both south and north, huge new temples and indeed extensive new sanctuaries were built, but the ziggurat of Ur is the best preserved of them all. Its base measured about 62·5 × 43 metres and it is estimated that the original height was about 20 metres. The shrine itself, of which no remains survive, was approached by a triple staircase, a central one leading straight up to the highest platform, while side stairways at right angles joined the main one on the terrace of the first stage of the tower. The ziggurat's mud core was enclosed by walls of baked brick bound with bitumen, each individual brick announcing in a neat stamped inscription that it was the work of 'Ur-nammu, king of Ur, who built the temple of Nanna'. The cult building itself, like that of other temples of this period, would probably have included an inner room with a platform at one end and a sacrificial table in the middle. In this chamber would take place the Sacred Marriage between Nanna and Gula (the goddess of childbirth). The Sacred Marriage between the city god or goddess and his or her consort was an important feature of Mesopotamian religion: enacted once or twice yearly with the roles being played by the king and a priestess, it was intended to ensure the fecundity of the city's fields, flocks and people.

The Mesopotamian temple, massively built and elaborately decorated in many colours, perched high on its artificial mountain above the city, must have dominated the people to whom it belonged and of whose corporate identity it was the symbol. The temple represented in the first place an enormous outlay of human effort. Falkenstein calculated that it would have taken 1,500 men, working a ten-hour day, five years to build one of the temple terraces at Uruk. The construction of the Mesopotamian temples was not done by slave labour. Though by late Early Dynastic times much temple building was run by the king, in the earlier periods it was done, in theory at least, by voluntary co-operative service. It was this dedication on the part of the individual to the service of the god that pro-vided the psychological motivation for the concentration both of man-power and of surplus food products and was one of the crucial factors in the accomplishment of the 'Urban Revolution'. The temple organization was run as a household: indeed the temple itself was regarded as the literal residence of the god. Every citizen belonged to one of the temples (originally there may have been a single temple for each settlement, but by the Early Dynastic period anyway each city seems to have housed several different temple communities) and the whole community, even the slaves, was referred to as 'the people of the god Nanna' (or whoever the deity in question was). The temple community comprised officials and priests, food-producers (farmers, herdsmen, fishermen), merchants, craftsmen (car-

The ziggurat, the platform within the temple precinct on which the shrine was raised, was the focal point of each Mesopotamian city. At Ur it stood 26 metres high (above and right). Uruk, where two settlements had been merged, boasted two ziggurats (below).

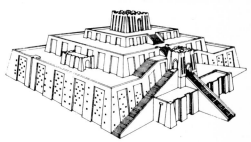

penters, potters, smiths, workers in leather, wool and basketry, stone-cutters), personnel involved directly in the upkeep of the temple establishment (bakers, brewers, gardeners) and slaves. As we have seen, many of these roles may have overlapped: in the beginning there were probably few full-time specialists. If we are right in what we have deduced about the nature of land ownership in Sumer, in the early phases the land was owned by the temple itself. One part was worked communally for the god, another part was divided into allotments and assigned to individuals for their own support, while a third type of land was let out to tenants for rent. Although there was some margin for the accumulation of private wealth, initially the vast bulk of agricultural and other produce passed through the temple magazines. As well as the products of Sumer itself, the goods from foreign trade—gold, silver, copper, lead, lapis lazuli, wood and so on—flowed straight into the temple stores. The merchants of Early Dynastic times were concerned exclusively with import and export; the distribution of goods within the community was organized by the temple (with a little scope for exchange between individuals on a barter basis). So the temple acted as the economic centre for the concentration and redistribution of goods. Even more importantly, it acted as the centre for the concentration and organization of labour: for work on the land, for the construction and upkeep of canals and dykes, for the construction and upkeep of the temple buildings themselves.

It was in order to deal with this centralized economic organization that writing was invented. Indeed when we look at the enormous bulk of administrative documents that Sumerian cities have yielded, we could be forgiven the impression that the Sumerians were a nation of book-keepers. Tallies and tokens, wage lists and ration lists, lists of supplies and monthly accounts—these are the documents we have in tens of thousands. The complexity of the temple organization was made greater by the fact that, though they had systems of weights and measures, to begin with they lacked money or indeed any constant exchange value, so that the accounts had to be balanced by the use of a series of approximate equations between the utility values of different commodities. For instance one *gur* of barley was considered equivalent to one *gin* of silver; it was also the rent for one *gan* of land (the precise values of these measures is unimportant for this purpose). Without writing, the administration of such a complex economic organization would surely have been impossible.

Although the central economic and social, as well as religious, power of the temple is indisputable, it does not seem to have been a political institution. By the time we have proper documents, i.e. during the Early Dynastic period, effective political power was in the hands of the king, and the Sumerian writers themselves clearly were unable to visualize a time before there were kings: to them kingship was a gift of the gods and of extremely remote antiquity. Yet some modern scholars hold different

War-leaders turned kings in Early Dynastic Sumer first shared then encroached upon the authority of the temple. They took control of public building for example, and the king above is shown with a basket of bricks on his head. They remained in direct command of the army (below), and helmeted guards (right) were found buried at the entrance to a king's tomb at Ur.

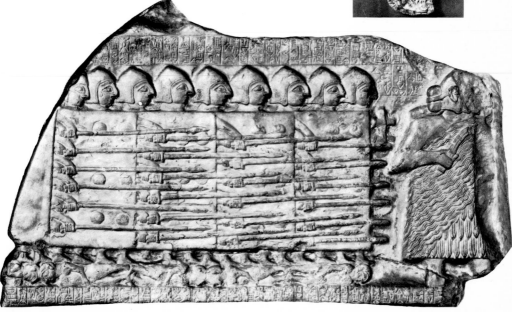

views: they believe that before the Early Dynastic period Sumer had what they call a 'primitive democracy'. Whether this was really the case is a matter of dispute, but the archaeological record, which attests so clearly the antiquity of the temple as an institution, equally clearly indicates that the institution of kingship was a relatively late development. This institution forms the subject of the next section.

The palace

Sumerian mythology has it that kingship was divine: it was first 'lowered from heaven' to the city of Eridu and after the Flood it was lowered again, this time to the city of Kish. As it happens, Kish is the city where we have the earliest archaeological indications of kingship—a royal palace—but this is no earlier than the Early Dynastic II period. There is another palace which is probably also of this period at Eridu and as well as the palaces we have, for the Early Dynastic period, what are clearly royal burials, both at Kish and in the famous 'Royal Cemetery' at Ur; probably contemporary too are the three large tombs found under the Ishtar temple at Mari in Syria. Before the Early Dynastic II period we have no archaeological evidence for the existence of kings and for the origin of the institution we must turn to the documents. Thorkild Jacobsen, who proposed the 'primitive democracy' idea, has argued that the Sumerian myths describing the world of the gods reflect political institutions of human society in the time before the rise of kings. From this starting point he goes on to suggest that political authority originally rested in an assembly of the adult male members of the community. This assembly would meet only in times of stress to elect a temporary war leader; eventually successful war leaders would retain power even in peace time, thus becoming the first kings. This theory is attractive for a number of reasons. Firstly, as I have said, the archaeological evidence indicates that kingship developed only at a rather late stage. Moreover the archaeological evidence also indicates a very close link between the palace and all military activity, which lends support to the idea of the origin of kings as war leaders. The term which came to be used to represent true kingship was *lugal*; it is used throughout the King List, for instance. Its literal meaning is 'great man' and it may originally have stood for the temporarily elected war leader. The other term often used for Sumerian rulers is *ensi* (in older accounts of this subject this used to be transliterated *patesi*) and this is often translated as 'governor'. However, the difference between the two titles is not really clear and may have altered with time; at least by the time of the Third Dynasty of Ur the *ensi* was undoubtedly a subsidiary official, appointed as governor by the national or imperial king, the *lugal*.

In the later phases of Mesopotamian civilization the palace became a parallel organization to the temple, owning vast landed estates and its

Among the sumptuous goods buried with the kings in the ▶
Royal Cemetery at Ur was this gold and lapis lazuli ram.

own workshops, stores and so on with a central administration collecting, storing and redistributing goods and concentrating and organizing labour. Unlike the Temple, however, it exacted military service, enforced labour on communal projects and levied direct taxes. In the early stages the palace was chiefly occupied with military activities which had no parallel in the temple organization—raising and supplying an army and constructing defensive walls around the city—and it never lost this military role: even in late Babylonian and Assyrian times the king was leader of the army in wartime. There was another difference too: the theoretically voluntary nature of work devoted to the god in the temple community was not paralleled in the palace organization. The famous Epic of Gilgamesh opens with the citizens protesting against their forced labour on the city walls. We have no comparable record (however mythical it may be) of complaints about the demands made for work in temple construction—though, as we have seen, the demands were very great—and it would probably have been unthinkable to complain about service to the god. This fact underlines one important difference between Sumerian and ancient Egyptian society: whereas Egyptian kings *were* gods and there was no separation between divine and royal power, Sumerian kings set up *in competition* with the gods. Of course they would not admit to such competition and, indeed, kings were quick to claim divine support for their activities, but the palace aped the temple in its organization and it grew in power at the expense of the temple.

As royal power grew, so did the more rigid stratification of society into classes. Although the origin of class stratification lay in the complex division of labour we find in the temple organization, the establishment of a palace elite—with a living human being and not a symbolic god as head of the community—provided the basis for the emergence of a much more rigid class structure, with far greater differences in wealth and status. We know from the documents that by the Old Babylonian period, early in the second millennium BC, there was a legally recognized division into three main classes: noblemen, commoners and slaves. For earlier periods, we do not have such clear documentary evidence, but the archaeological record demonstrates the increasing differentiation in wealth and status and its association with the royal household. The clearest evidence comes from a study of the goods placed with the dead in their graves. From prehistoric times until Early Dynastic II–III graves were well provided with pottery vessels, presumably containing food and drink, but metal goods and jewellery were comparatively rare, more elaborate furniture totally absent. In the later Early Dynastic cemeteries the majority of graves still have only vases; some have the occasional copper vessel or necklace of precious beads, but only a very small proportion—the royal tombs—are really lavishly equipped. At Mari under the Temple of Ishtar (the Semitic name for the Sumerian goddess of love, Inanna), at Kish in

◄ *Mes-kalam-dug was buried at Ur in ritual military dress, his helmet beaten from a single sheet of 15-carat gold.*

the so-called Y cemetery and in the Royal Cemetery at Ur there were subterranean chambers built in stone and baked brick and roofed with corbelled vaults. The royal corpses were often buried with one or more four-wheeled wagons or two-wheeled chariots; accompanying these vehicles were the bodies of the oxen which drew them and, in several tombs, the bodies of the attendants who had served the royal family in life. The most spectacular example of this practice of *sati* burial is in the 'King's Grave' in the Royal Cemetery at Ur, where up to 63 people were buried in the shaft by which the burial chamber is approached: they included drivers, soldiers, courtiers, musicians and women decked out in costly jewellery (either ladies-in-waiting or courtesans). Up till recently no reference to the practice of *sati* burial had been found in the tablets, but such a reference has now been found in a document entitled 'The Death of Gilgamesh'. It is not found either archaeologically or in the tablets after the end of the Early Dynastic period and it is doubtful whether Mesopotamian society could have afforded such wastage of its human resources—whatever the social value of the display—as a regular practice.

From the Royal Cemetery at Ur came some of the most famous antiquities of the Sumerian world, a few of which I reproduce here to illustrate the splendour of these goods. The so-called 'Royal Standard' of Ur is perhaps the best-known object from ancient Mesopotania; it is probably in fact the sound box of a musical instrument. It is an oblong wooden box with an inlay of shell, limestone and lapis lazuli, set in bitumen. The lapis lazuli forms a blue background to figures in shell and limestone in contrasting scenes of War and Peace. Made of gold and lapis lazuli are the figure of a ram against a flowering shrub and a bull's head (also part of a musical instrument). Of gold alone is the helmet of Mes-kalam-dug and the goblet and bowl of queen Puabi (formerly Shub-ad). Gold, silver, copper and lapis lazuli were all used in abundance and they are all materials, we must remember, that had to be imported into Sumer. Indeed one of the effects of the rise of royal dynasties was a great increase in the demand for and the production of non-agricultural goods and presumably a corresponding increase in the number of full-time specialists engaged in acquiring the materials (merchants) and making the goods (craftsmen). In the wake of the demand from the royal household (for luxury goods) and the military establishment (for armaments), a private demand for non-essential goods grew up. In the later part of the Early Dynastic period we can recognize the existence of at least a small middle class. If it was the temple that provided the mechanism for the initial development of urban society in Mesopotamia, it was the rise of the palace that turned it into a consumer society.

The enormous wealth of the palace was clearly reflected at Ur in a queen's tomb as well. There, with queen Pu-abi, were found these solid gold vessels, the goblet (right) with traces of green eye-paint in it.

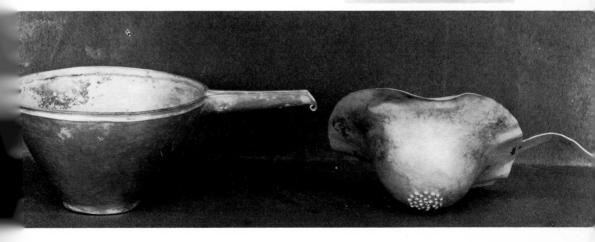

Subsistence economy

As we have already mentioned and shall return to again, Mesopotamian civilization, like its contemporaries in Egypt and the Indus plain, was built on intensive cereal production on irrigated land. While both wheat and barley were grown, barley with its greater tolerance of salt was always the more important crop and seems to have replaced wheat altogether by the end of the third millennium BC. It was customary to harvest two crops a year, but this was sometimes reduced to one in an attempt to combat the effects of the increasing salinity of the soil. It was only the production of high yields of cereals that could support an urban population and it was only through irrigation that such yields could be obtained. Irrigation was therefore a crucial function in Mesopotamia and, unlike the situation in Egypt, it was not a simple matter of allowing natural flood water freely on to the land. The Mesopotamian rivers flood in March and April when enormous quantities of water pour down from the mountains; by contrast, in the following summer months water is in short supply. It is necessary to retain the water in spring and to let it out in the summer. In fact a large part of the irrigation water came not from stored up flood water but from what flowed in the rivers at all times of year. As a result of the constant deposition of silt over long periods the rivers flowed at a level above that of the fields and this facilitated the carriage of water over great distances, since it could be propelled simply by gravity. However, the work involved in building the canals was immense and they needed constant maintenance: the banks had to be repaired and strengthened annually to prevent breaching at flood time and the channels had to be constantly cleared of silt. Though probably originally the temple's task, at least by 2500 BC the construction of the main canals had become the responsibility of the king and inscriptions make it clear that these works were as important for royal prestige as military victories or the construction of temples.

While barley was undoubtedly the main crop, the Sumerian subsistence economy was varied. Many other plant foods were grown: the most important was the date palm, with its tolerance of salinity and its high food value (dates are a valuable source of iron in the diet, as well as having a high sugar content). Other fruits grown included apples, cherries, plums, peaches, pomegranates, figs, grapes and melons. Among the vegetables, pulses such as peas and lentils were accompanied by onions, lettuce and cucumbers and a variety of herbs and spices.

The animal side of the diet was provided both by domesticated animals and from wild food sources. Goats and sheep were the most important of the domesticated animals. Many different words for sheep appear in the documents (31 already in the protoliterate phase) and they were certainly selectively bred, presumably for the wool, which, woven into cloth, provided one of Sumer's most important exports. Both sheep

The land's high yield in Mesopotamia allowed some to farm, others to fish (left) or to hunt, and the temple was the centre of redistribution of supplies (below). A temple frieze (top) reflects a preoccupation with matters of subsistence. Onagers (above), donkeys and oxen were harnessed or used as pack animals.

and goats were used for the production of dairy foods—milk, butter and cheese—as were the smaller number of cattle. Swine were popular in Sumerian times, but went out of favour with the Semitic dominance of Mesopotamia. As well as their use for food, cattle (the castrated males, the oxen) were used to pull ploughs and wagons as well as boats. Onagers, donkeys and camels were used for traction and riding or as pack animals, but were probably not eaten.

The wild food resources of Mesopotamia were rich: all the waterways and the sea to the south abounded in fish and the marshland at the head of the Gulf sheltered many varieties of game birds and animals. Throughout the plain deer and gazelle were hunted. And, finally, wild honey was gathered, though the Sumerians, unlike the Egyptians, did not keep bees.

The Sumerians' subsistence economy was that of their prehistoric ancestors, altered only by increasing efficiency: a difference not of kind but of degree.

Technology and crafts

In this section we are dealing with two different though related fields. On the one hand we are concerned with major technological innovations that had important economic and social implications and, on the other, with the level of technical proficiency and artistry in craft practice. In the story of the civilization of southern Mesopotamia the high points of development in these two fields occupy different chronological positions. The major developments in technology belong to the prehistoric or protoliterate phases, that is to say they precede the full crystallization of civilization, while the flowering of skill and artistry in production belongs to the Early Dynastic period.

The major technological achievements that preceded the 'Urban Revolution' included the discovery of metallurgy, the invention of the wheel and the harnessing of animal and wind power. Metallurgy indeed has a great antiquity in the Near East. We now know that true smelted copper was in use as early as the seventh millennium bc in Anatolia and by the fifth millennium bc it was in general use in Mesopotamia, Palestine and Iran. Interestingly enough, in Mesopotamia it was used more in the north than in the south. The northern Halafian culture was already metal-using and the succeeding Ubaid phase in the north is marked by the appearance of cast copper axes and the first use of gold. By contrast there is very little evidence for the use of metal by Ubaid people in the south (in Sumer proper), though there is just enough to deduce that they definitely knew copper. The reason for this geographical divergence is probably simply that northern Mesopotamia is much closer to sources of copper than the south.

Definite evidence for the use of the wheel comes in the late Uruk period. The pictograms on the tablets from Uruk IV depict indisputable wheeled vehicles. Whether they existed in even earlier phases is at present unknown. However, the potter's wheel was in use from the beginning of the Uruk period (Uruk XIV), so the principle of the wheel was certainly known from this time. Wheeled vehicles, needless to say, revolutionized transport, but the use of the potter's wheel was also of considerable significance: ethnographic parallels suggest that, whereas hand-made pottery is normally a domestic product, wheel-made pottery is more often produced industrially (by at least part-time specialists). Probably the appearance of the potter's wheel in Uruk times indicates that this significant step in the development of economic specialization had been taken.

The harnessing of animal and wind power probably also preceded the emergence of full civilization. The wind had been exploited for water transport by late Ubaid times since a grave of this period at Eridu has yielded a model of a sailing boat—the oldest yet documented anywhere. We do not know precisely when animals were put to pulling carts or ploughs, but they were certainly used for this purpose by the Uruk stage when we have evidence for both oxen and onagers being used in this way.

These are of course not all the important technological achievements characteristic of Sumerian civilization, but they are among the most important and I have chosen to discuss them because we do have definite evidence for their chronological position *before* (and in some if not all cases a long time before) civilization developed fully.

The late prehistoric and the protoliterate periods appear in the archaeological record as phases of rapid and creative technological development, with advances in the manufacture of, among other things, seals, metal tools and stone and metal vessels. By contrast the Early Dynastic period appears technologically not as a period of invention but rather as a period of consolidation and expansion based on the achievements of the earlier period. However, quantitatively there was an enormous increase in production in Early Dynastic times; indeed this was an important feature of the growing urban economy, with production stimulated largely by the royal retinue and the growing military establishment. This increase in production indicates an increase in the number of full-time specialist craftsmen with both the time and the opportunity to develop a high level of skill in their crafts. Their achievements are most easily recognized archaeologically in the field of metallurgy. The Sumerian smiths knew not only copper, silver, gold and lead, but they occasionally even employed iron; they alloyed copper with lead and, by Early Dynastic III times at least, also with tin to produce bronze. They had mastered the techniques of casting by the *cire perdue* method, of producing beaten sheet metal, of rivetting, brazing and using lead as a solder; they also

77

made socketed tools which may have been the first such tools anywhere. The Sumerian jewellers too practised gold-beating, casting, soldering, chasing and filigree work, sometimes of great delicacy. Equally accomplished were the seal-cutters and stone-workers and the faïence and glass-workers (indeed true glass was another Sumerian invention). Of wooden and textile products little survives but we know from the documents that textiles in particular were produced in quantity and enormous variety for export and we may assume a high level of skill in these crafts too. We have seen already, in our discussion of the Early Dynastic shrine at al'Ubaid, how the Sumerian craftsmen favoured scenes created by inlaying stone and shell figures in a bitumen background. This inlay technique was also used for smaller objects including the most famous of all Sumerian products, the 'Royal Standard' of Ur. This and the other fine objects from the Royal Cemetery of Ur represent the highest point of Sumerian craft skill.

Thus, as Robert Adams has pointed out, the major quantitative growth of metallurgy and other specialized crafts occurred only after civilization was well established and indeed he regards technological expansion as 'less a cause than a consequence of city growth'. However, it is probably true that the major technological innovations with which we began this discussion—the *discovery* of metallurgy, the invention of the wheel and the harnessing of animal and wind power—were necessary preconditions for the development of civilization. It is certainly the case that they did precede the Early Dynastic phase of Mesopotamian civilization.

Trade

As we have already seen, the southern Mesopotamian plain is totally lacking in mineral resources and in good timber. All the materials necessary for the support and embellishment of civilized life had to be imported into Sumer. Of the metals, copper came from Oman (at the southern end of the Persian Gulf) and from the Taurus mountains of Anatolia, gold from Elam and Syria, and silver and lead from Elam and from Anatolia, which also produced a little iron. The source of the tin used by the Sumerians is unknown; the most plausible suggestions are Anatolia and eastern Iran. Oman produced volcanic rocks used for quern stones and for statues, while soapstone was imported from the southern part of the Iranian plateau. Mother-of-pearl came from the Persian Gulf, sank shells from India, amber and carnelian from Anatolia and perhaps the Persian Gulf, while lapis lazuli, highly prized in Mesopotamia as in Egypt for its bright blue colour, was brought all the way from the Badakshan area of northern Afghanistan. Timber was imported both from the Zagros mountains to the east and from the Lebanon to the west. What

Sumerian craftsmen work-
ed in silver (above), in
copper (right), in bronze,
gold, lead and even iron.
They were accomplished
in inlay in all materials
(below left and far below).
They were potters (below
right).

the Sumerian cities drew from these distant zones and what they needed in vast quantities was raw materials: very few manufactured goods were imported. For the whole of the Early Dynastic period there are only a few seals imported from the Indus Valley civilization and some stone vases probably imported from the Makran; for the period of Sargon there are a few more imports, but still only a very small number and still only from the same two sources, the Indus Valley and the Makran. Interestingly enough no Egyptian objects have been found in Sumer, though a few Mesopotamian goods have turned up in the Nile Valley. In exchange for the raw materials that they needed so badly, the Sumerians exported manufactured goods. Sumerian seals and other small objects turn up in archaeological excavations in several areas of western Asia, but the documents suggest that the most important exports were textiles, which were produced in great quantities in the temple and royal workshops.

We know something about the way in which the trade was carried out, at least in the later periods, through the fortunate discovery of a Mesopotamian trading post at Kanesh (Kultepe) in Anatolia. The tablets excavated on this site (amounting to more than 16,000 texts, of which only 2,000 have been published) are written in the cuneiform script and the Akkadian language. They record the commercial transactions of the community of Assyrian merchants who occupied a walled cantonment on the outskirts of the native city. Some people believe that the colony may have been established as early as 2500 BC, but the tablets examined so far belong to the two and a half centuries following 2000 BC. The colony, known as a *karum* or *karu*, was one of seven or eight established in Anatolia, but it seems to have been the most important and it is the only one of which the site has been found. The trade was organized by a series of small family 'firms' apparently acting independently, but all working directly for the royal or temple organization at home (in the case of Kanesh the home city was Assur). The *karum* has been described as a sort of 'Chamber of Commerce' controlling the mechanism of trade between Assyria and Anatolia. It was responsible for the dispatch of caravans and their safe conduct and for the payment of dues. The tablets represent a business correspondence, comprising bills-of-lading, accounts and records of litigation. Each consignment of goods from Mesopotamia had to pass through the palace of the native ruler, who could exercise an option to buy or else would levy taxes. The tablets make it clear that textiles were the main export from Mesopotamia, copper from Anatolia. Goods were carried by donkey; wheeled vehicles were probably *not* used. It is interesting, and indeed impressive, that there seem to have been few problems in protecting these precious consignments from bandits on their long overland journey. Although the documents make no mention of it, it seems probable that military protection was available for these caravans both in Mesopotamia and in Anatolia.

Childe emphasized the important role played by trade in the accomplishment of the Urban Revolution. In the alluvial valleys the economic self-sufficiency which was possible in the highland zones and which had been characteristic of the earliest farming communities in western Asia could not be maintained. Some regular system of trade had to be organized to secure supplies not just of luxuries, but of *essential* raw materials. The fertility of the soil in the valleys allowed the production of sufficient surplus food to satisfy this need for imports, but it led to the emergence of an entirely new economic structure with a body of merchants not themselves engaged in primary production but supported out of the surplus produced by those who were. Economic specialization was one of the crucial factors in the development of civilization and the necessity for importing raw materials was one of the two pillars on which the new economic structure was erected (the other being the nature of the subsistence economy itself). Thus, paradoxically, one of Sumer's apparent disadvantages—its lack of mineral resources—contributed vitally to the flowering of civilization in the region.

Chapter V   Mesopotamia: the Fruits of Civilization

The development of urban life opened up many new avenues of human activity. In this chapter I shall deal with education, law, religious beliefs, the creative arts and theoretical knowledge. All of these are known to us mainly through the written documents and I shall begin with a discussion of writing itself.

Writing

Writing is a characteristic trait of all the south-west Asian civilizations and is often by itself taken as a criterion by which we can define civilization (although the American civilizations were either illiterate or had only a very limited system of writing). The Sumerians were probably the first to develop writing—the earliest Mesopotamian tablets go back to about 3500 BC—though the Proto-Elamite script of Iran might be equally early. The Egyptian hieroglyphic system probably emerged a few centuries later, with the still undeciphered Indus script slightly later still. Whether the practice of writing was diffused from a single centre (presumably Sumer) or was developed independently in several different places is a subject of fervent controversy, which I shall return to in chapter 9. Here I am concerned with the development of writing in Mesopotamia.

Historians of Mesopotamia are fortunate in that the writing material used in the Land between the Rivers was from the beginning clay and not a perishable material such as papyrus, parchment, leather or wood. The Mesopotamian clay tablets, dried in the sun or sometimes baked, endure almost for ever in the arid climatic conditions of the land; and we thus have tens of thousands of tablets from the Sumerian period alone and something like half a million from the later Mesopotamian civilizations. We also have short inscriptions on stone seals (and on clay sealings), and inscriptions on stone (on statues and monuments), on bricks and on precious metal vessels, but the majority of Sumerian writing is on clay tablets.

The earliest writing belongs to the Uruk period, before about 3500 BC. The first written 'document' we have is a tablet not of clay but of limestone, from Kish, bearing crudely formed incised pictographic signs. This probably belongs to the early Uruk period, whereas a collection of several hundred tablets from the site of Uruk itself belong to the late Uruk phase. These tablets from Uruk bear scratched signs, which, like those on the Kish stone tablet, are *pictographic* in nature: each sign represents a single object or action and is indeed simply a picture, necessarily rather stylized, of the object or action in question. By the succeeding protoliterate period the script was no longer purely pictographic, but *ideographic*: the literal meaning of the original pictogram might be expanded to represent general ideas associated with it. For example, the symbol for 'star' came to stand also for 'heaven' and 'god'. A further development that had already occurred by this stage was that the script had become partly phonetically based; some signs now stood not only directly for the original object depicted (or an idea directly associated with it), but also, by extension, for the *sound* of the Sumerian word for that object or idea. Thus the sign depicting 'arrow' came to represent also the sound pattern *ti* (i.e. the Sumerian word for 'arrow') in general. Accordingly, the same sign could then be used for quite a different and unrelated lexical word *ti*, this time meaning 'life'. In a similar fashion, the sign originally depicting 'water' (*a*) could be extended to represent *a* in general, and could thus again be used for another unrelated lexical word, this time the preposition 'in' (also *a*). By this process of extension, Sumerian was able eventually to assemble a complete *syllabary*, i.e. a system of written signs, phonetically based, in which, ideally, each sign represented a separate sound sequence or syllable.

Unfortunately, this syllabary fell short, as indeed do all modern alphabetic systems, of the ideal standard of a one-to-one relationship between phonetic sounds and written symbols. Just as the original ideograms could depict several objects or ideas, visually or conceptually related (as, for instance, one sign depicting, as appropriate, 'face', 'speak', 'cry' or 'word'), so too these same signs, when used phonetically, could end up with several possible sets of values. The difficulty was, of course, that the visual and conceptual connection would not be paralleled by any connection between the respective phonetic shapes of the *words* for these objects and ideas (*ka*, *dug*, *gug* and *enim* in the example quoted in the previous sentence).

Possibly as a means of relieving this resulting ambiguity, some ideograms were retained as *determinatives* and attached to individual words to aid the reader's interpretation. Thus names of deities would be accompanied by the deity sign (⋈⊢), names of stones by the stone sign (▨⧧), and types of skin and leather by another sign (⋈⊨𝍡).

Sumerian writing was first made up of pictograms, each representing a single subject (col. 1). Set down in columns or in individual squares, they were drawn in soft clay or scratched on stone. Ideograms followed, with extra meanings attached to the original pictogram. 'Star' now also stood for 'heaven' and 'god'. Signs began to be set down horizontally and were rotated (col. 2). Later a wedge-shaped tool was used to make impressions in the clay that bore less and less relationship to the pictograms from which they were derived (cols. 3, 4).

The transition to this stage may have been made easier by the fact that Sumerian tends by nature to monosyllabic roots. Such polysyllabic words as occur would of course be represented by the appropriate succession of syllables. This conversion from ideographic to phonetic script may also have been accelerated, in Mesopotamia, by the need that arose in the middle of the third millennium BC to transcribe in the script invented for Sumerian a second and unrelated language, the Semitic Akkadian tongue.

On the earliest tablets the signs were inscribed vertically, but by the protoliterate period the direction of writing had changed to the horizontal (running from left to right, as we ourselves write) and the pictograms were rotated, so that they seemed to be lying on their backs. The early symbols, pictograms or ideograms, were scratched on the clay with a pointed stylus (originally a marsh reed); subsequently a stylus with a blunter end was employed and the signs were impressed instead of scratched, producing characteristic wedge-shaped marks. The word *cuneiform* comes from the Latin *cuneus* (a wedge) and *forma* (shape) and describes the script that was used from Early Dynastic times until the last few centuries BC, both for the Sumerian and the Akkadian languages and was indeed adapted for several others used in neighbouring countries (e.g. Hittite). The cuneiform signs were formed of clusters of wedge-shaped strokes and as such were necessarily highly stylized, so that as time passed they became increasingly less like the pictograms from which they were derived.

For reasons that are apparent, pictographic and ideographic scripts have to have enormous numbers of symbols if they are to be used for more than the most rudimentary functions (Chinese, which uses a script of this type, has tens of thousands of symbols, of which 3,000–5,000 are in relatively common use). Syllabic scripts can manage with a much smaller number of symbols, but they still generally use several hundreds, whereas alphabetic scripts are by far the most economical, needing no more than 22–26 separate symbols. Thus we might expect decreasing numbers of symbols on the Mesopotamian tablets as the script developed and this is in fact the case: the earliest pictographic tablets use more than 2,000 signs, which were eventually reduced to 600–700 by Babylonian times, of which about 300 were still ideograms.

As we have seen, all the earliest Sumerian tablets and very many of the later ones are temple archives and there is no doubt that the Mesopotamian system of writing was developed in order to cope with the complex book-keeping required by the temple communities. As time progressed writing was employed also for more detailed administrative and legal documents. Kings adopted it at an early stage for the purpose of issuing royal edicts and to record, often in monumental form, their achievements for posterity. It was not for something like a millennium after the first simple lists and accounts were made that writing began to be used for anything that we might describe as creative and it was still later before the new means of communication was employed to impart knowledge, whether of craft practice or theoretical 'science'. We are inclined to think today of writing as a means of transmitting human experience across both chronological and geographical barriers: we think of personal correspondence, of newspapers, of literature and poetry and of scientific journals. However, in the fourth and early third millennia BC the potential of the new means of communication was latent; its uses were humble and strictly utilitarian.

The tablets

The Sumerian clay tablets can be divided into a number of classes. The earliest tablets we have and indeed the vast majority of documents of all periods are economic and administrative. As we have already seen, it was the demands of an increasingly complex economic system that called forth the invention of writing. The earliest tablets were either small labels originally attached to containers and recording the type and quantity of material they contained or larger tablets inscribed with lists of types and quantities of commodities. Rather later we find more elaborate accounts, ration lists, allotment lists, wage lists and so on. Until the middle of the third millennium BC these documents occur only in the temple complexes and at this stage writing may have been practised exclusively in the service of the temple. The sites of Uruk, Shuruppak and Lagash have produced particularly extensive collections of tablets from their temple complexes. Those from Uruk come from the Predynastic period; those from Shuruppak mainly from the early part of the Early Dynastic period, while those from Lagash come from the late Early Dynastic period and later periods. Later on, in the early second millennium BC, we have the exceptional collection of many thousands of commercial texts from the Assyrian colony at Kanesh in Anatolia: these comprise bills-of-lading, accounts, letters and legal documents which throw invaluable light on the nature of Mesopotamian trade.

The primary book-keeping function of the written word was appreciated by the Sumerians themselves and they clearly felt that the divine world must have functioned in the same way. It is in this context that we can understand several references in the texts to the scribe of the ruler of the underworld who kept lists bearing the names of all those who were to die each day: clearly the underworld had to keep its records straight!

The second main group of tablets comprises legal documents. Mesopotamian civilization is famous for its law codes—so much so that the name of Hammurabi, king of Babylon in the first half of the eighteenth century BC, is familiar to every school child as that of the world's first law-giver. This is in fact incorrect: the earliest law code we have, that of

The bulk of Sumerian writing was done on clay tablets, like this account of fields and crops from Jamdat Nasr. ▶

Ur-nammu, is almost three centuries earlier than that of Hammurabi and we have evidence of the existence of regular laws much earlier. However, we are right to think of the ancient Mesopotamians as much preoccupied with legal matters. As well as the actual codes of law, we have innumerable legal documents: deeds of sale, contracts and records of litigation. The nature of Sumerian laws will be discussed later, but two interesting general impressions emerge from their study. One is that we are clearly dealing with human rules of behaviour and not divine laws, in contrast to the Mosaic code, for example. Although the rulers associated with the law codes we have (Ur-nammu, Lipit-ishtar and Hammurabi) were careful to claim divine support and we know that all parties to and witnesses involved in lawsuits were bound by religious oaths administered in the temple itself, there is no suggestion that the laws themselves were divine and immutable. On the contrary, the Mesopotamian rulers regarded their laws as capable of emendation and improvement and indeed were proud to claim such improvements as achievements. One of the most fascinating documents referring to law and, incidentally, one of the earliest is the so-called Urukagina reform document. Urukagina was king of Lagash in the middle of the twenty-fourth century BC and he seems to have been responsible for a series of sweeping legal reforms, correcting a variety of abuses stemming from a corrupt and over-powerful palace bureaucracy. Many specific abuses are listed and the scribe records a complaint that seems most familiar to us today: 'from the borders of Ningursu [the patron deity of Lagash] to the sea, there was the tax collector'! This is followed by a list of the reforms effected by Urukagina, after which— 'from the borders of Ningursu to the sea, there was no tax collector'.

The second impression to emerge from the study of the Mesopotamian legal documents is the high regard in which the written word was held. Clearly, just as we today need our 'pieces of paper' to prove that we are legally married or divorced, owners of our houses, qualified for our jobs, entitled to drive a car and so on, so the ancient Mesopotamians needed their clay tablets to invest their activities with appropriate legal status. However, in Sumer this was probably true of only a very small section of the community.

Sacred and literary texts record the traditions and beliefs of Meso-potamian society and comprise myths, epics, hymns and lamentations. Essays and proverbs form a more prosaic, related group of texts. These are among the most interesting of all the Sumerian documents and have been the subject of much concentrated study, especially in the last quarter of a century. We have perhaps 5,000 tablets or fragments that fall into this class, the vast majority coming from the sanctuary of Enlil at Nippur, the religious centre of Sumer. The earliest go back to about 2400 BC, but the high point of Sumerian literary development belonged to the end of the third millennium BC, under the Third Dynasty of Ur. We are fortunate

Inscriptions were set up in public places. Here a monument to Naram-sin of Agade celebrates his victories in pictures and in writing.

that the Babylonians and Assyrians took over the Sumerian literary tradition complete, since much of our knowledge of Sumerian literature comes from later copies of Sumerian texts, not yet discovered in their early form.

Though truly objective historical accounts are unknown in ancient Mesopotamia, we have a number of texts which were broadly historical in intention. These include the King List already discussed and many votive and dedicatory inscriptions, some quite elaborate. One of the most famous is an account of a prolonged war between the cities of Lagash and Umma over the ownership of a disputed piece of territory known as the Guedinna. It dates from the twenty-fourth century BC.

We have virtually no scientific or scholarly texts for the Sumerian period proper, but by Old Babylonian times we find accurate descriptions of the autopsies performed by the special class of priests known as diviners, whose job it was to interpret the gods' intentions from examination of animal entrails. Astronomical texts appear only in the first millennium BC. One Sumerian tablet we have that can claim to be truly scientific predates 2000 BC and contains fifteen medical prescriptions; interestingly enough it is totally free from spells or incantations though these abound in the medical texts of later periods.

Texts used in the schools for training scribes comprise word lists, grammar 'books', mathematical tables and mathematical problems. They will be discussed in more detail in the next section.

Ritual texts include, on a monumental level, foundation tablets and ceremonial inscriptions carved on mountain sides and, on a personal level, inscribed amulets and phylacteries. The texts are addressed not to human beings but to gods or to the supernatural world in general; this does not, of course, stop them from providing us incidentally with much useful historical and other information.

Education

Along with the invention of writing went the development of a formal system of education—aimed, however, only at the very small proportion of the population destined to be literate. Of course if the scribe had to learn 2,000 signs or more, as he did in the early stages, an organized system of education was essential. Indeed the very early group of pictographic tablets from Uruk includes a few word lists intended for teaching purposes and these lists remained a feature of Mesopotamian 'libraries' at all periods. Although these rudimentary 'text-books' are found from the beginning, most of our evidence for Sumerian schools comes from the second half of the third and the first half of the second millennium BC. The original aim of the Sumerian school, known as *edubba* (literally tablet house) was undoubtedly to train the civil service that ran the temple and

Tablets of the Uruk period (above) bear the earliest pictographic writing of Mesopotamia. An Early Dynastic foundation tablet (top right), of the temple at al'Ubaid, attempts cuneiform. Seal impressions of succeeding periods —Akkadian, 3rd Dynasty of Ur and Old Babylonian (right) —carry inscriptions in the developing cuneiform. The foundation inscription on a bronze cone (below) would probably have been hidden from sight, driven into the fabric of the temple.

palace organizations, but as time passed they became also centres of scholarship and of creative writing. The schoolboy's work (and incidentally there were no schoolgirls: only boys were educated) consisted mostly of copying tablets prepared by the teacher: the primary aim was to learn to read and write the Sumerian language and later the Akkadian language also. We have 'text-books' which list names of trees and flowers, animals, birds and insects, stones and minerals, towns and villages, but these were prepared not to teach the students botany, zoology, geology or geography, but simply to teach him the large number of words he needed to know. We have bilingual texts, mostly word lists, in Akkadian and Sumerian (which incidentally played a crucial role in the initial decipherment of the Sumerian language) and simple Sumerian grammars.

Mathematics does seem to have been studied as a subject in its own right, but not in the modern way, starting from general theory. The Sumerian mathematical texts are of two different kinds. On the one hand there is a series of tables, like our own multiplication tables, designed to be memorized in order to facilitate simple arithmetical calculations. The other texts are concrete examples of actual mathematical problems worked out in full. It is not clear whether the Sumerians were unable to formulate the principles behind these problems (which they clearly understood in practice) or whether, alternatively, this part of the instruction was done orally, using the texts as examples.

Some students at least must have learnt such specialist topics as medicine or divination. We know this is the case because we have the texts used for such instruction, but we do not know what degree of educational specialization there was or how it was organized.

All students studied Sumerian literature, but this took the form largely of studying, copying and imitating ancient texts. Indeed this respect for ancient authorities was so deeply ingrained in all aspects of Mesopotamian education—including the 'scientific' ones—that it seems remarkable that new works were ever written. There do in fact seem to have been creative periods in Mesopotamian history, but, although it seems clear that they must have originated in the schools, it is not certain in what context new works were conceived. It is worth making the point here that all Sumerian writing was social, not personal: although a few texts give us glimpses of individual experience, these are incidental to the purpose of the text. There can have been no parallel in ancient Mesopotamia to the modern artist who puts his private experience into words (or pictures, or anything else).

We do not know where the Sumerian schools were or what they looked like. Only one excavated building has been tentatively interpreted as a school: it is at Mari and it consists of two rooms containing several rows of benches made of baked brick. We do not know who taught in the schools or who paid the teachers. We might guess that in the early stages the school was part of the temple organization, but we have no proof of this. We know that only boys were educated and from documents of about 2000 BC we know that they were the sons of wealthy and respected citizens: governors, ambassadors, temple administrators, army officers, sea captains, high tax officials, priests, managers, supervisors, foremen, scribes, archivists and accountants. Of course many of these categories of occupation did not exist in the earlier period, but we should probably be right to assume that scribes came from and remained part of a privileged section of the community from an early stage.

Law

We have seen that the Mesopotamian clay tablets contain many records of legal transactions as well as transcriptions of actual law codes. From these sources we know much about Sumerian laws and about the way justice was administered. The law codes were probably all inscribed on stone slabs, originally set up in a prominent public position, but only one such 'stele' has been found—that bearing the famous law code of Hammurabi (1792–1750 BC), now in the Louvre, which was found in the city of Susa in south-west Iran, where it had been carried as war booty by victorious Elamite raiders. The earlier law codes, such as those of Ur-nammu and Lipit-ishtar are known only from clay tablets, but these may have been copies of originals inscribed on stone stelae.

From the important Urukagina reform text already mentioned (c. 2350 BC), through the law codes of Ur-nammu (2112–2095 BC), an unnamed one from the city of Eshnunna, the code of Lipit-ishtar (1934–1924 BC) and Hammurabi (1792–1750 BC) to the Middle Assyrian laws of about 1450–1250 BC we can trace to some extent the development of Mesopotamian law as a whole. In the earliest stages for which we have records the laws seem by our standards to be rather progressive. Although both capital and corporal punishment existed for some offences, most punishment took the form of money fines, even for crimes of violence. The Ur-nammu code, for instance, specifies that '. . . if a man has severed with a weapon the bones of another man . . . he shall pay one mina of silver' and the slightly later code from the city of Eshnunna prescribes '. . . if a man bites a man's nose and severs it, he shall pay one mina of silver; for an eye one mina; for a tooth half a mina'. By the time of Hammurabi this had changed: the Babylonian laws, unlike the Sumerian, adopt the 'eye for an eye, tooth for a tooth' principle, which is so familiar to us from the Old Testament. The Hammurabi code in fact goes further than this in the direction of severity. Capital punishment (by drowning, burning or impaling) or various severe mutilations were prescribed for a variety of crimes including thefts with violence, sexual offences such as rape, incest, adultery and abortion and other crimes, including perjury, kidnapping and aiding slaves to escape. By Middle Assyrian times the tendency towards brutal physical punishments had intensified and it is clear that the Assyrians well deserved their ancient reputation for cruelty. One Middle Assyrian law reads '. . . if a woman has crushed a gentleman's testicle in a brawl, they shall cut off one of her fingers and if the other testicle has become affected . . . or she has crushed the other testicle in a brawl, they shall tear out both her eyes'—which casts some interesting light not only on Assyrian law but on social behaviour of the period!

We have evidence of Sumerian laws referring to marriage, divorce, adoption, support of children, inheritance, sale of property and slaves. Indeed the earliest known legal documents concern the sale of slaves, while the sale of fields and houses, though attested occasionally before the Third Dynasty of Ur, became common only from the Old Babylonian period, by which time private enterprise was playing an important role in the economy. From Old Babylonian times we have also laws connected with trade and commerce, for which we have no evidence in the earlier periods.

By the time of Hammurabi, men were not all equal before the law. His code recognizes three classes: gentlemen (*awilum*), commoners (*mushkenum*) and slaves (*wardum*), with different legal obligations and status. An offence against a gentleman was punished more severely than the same offence against a commoner: for instance, the accidental killing of a gentleman cost half a mina, that of a commoner only one third of a mina. Conversely, if the gentleman was the guilty party he was punished more severely than a commoner would have been. The earlier law codes contain no such clear identification of social classes and it may be that in Sumerian times the class system had not yet crystallized out in such a rigid form.

Most of our information on the actual administration of justice comes from the period of the Third Dynasty of Ur and is derived from a series of court records excavated at Lagash. By this stage the administration of law was in the hands of the *ensis*, the local rulers of the city states. There are some slight indications that there were separate ecclesiastical courts in the temples and we may guess that at an early stage the administration of justice, like almost all other 'state' functions, was in the hands of the temple. By the end of the third millennium BC, however, the only role played by the temple in legal practice was as the place where the oaths which bound the litigants and witnesses were administered. The plaintiff applied in the first instance to the *mashkim*, a sort of clerk of the court, whose job it was to prepare the case for court and to deal with court procedure during the case. The court consisted of one to four judges (usually three or four) called *dikud*. Neither the judges nor the *mashkim*'s positions were professional posts: they were held by respected citizens of various professions—temple administrators, scribes, archivists or city

94

The Mesopotamians were keen law-makers. Codes of law are known from as early as the Third Dynasty of Ur and were drawn up by the palace not the temple. A version of the laws of the city of Eshnunna is shown above and Hammurabi's laws for Babylon (right) have survived on the column on which they were inscribed for public display.

elders for instance—rather like our own Justices of the Peace. There is some indication that the *mashkim* was paid for his services; we do not know whether the judges received any remuneration.

The suit was initiated by one of the parties. The testimony might consist of statements made by witnesses under oath or by one of the parties under oath; or it might take the form of written documents or statements made by 'experts' or important officials. Once recorded in writing, the sentence could not be reversed, but there is some evidence that there was a higher court of appeal based at Nippur: one document refers to the 'seven royal judges of Nippur'. By the time of Hammurabi there was certainly a higher court, known as the 'Judges of Babylon'. The sentence was carried out by constables attached to the court. A summary of the case, the verdict and the sentence, together with the names of everyone involved was inscribed on a special tablet known as a *ditilla*, which was authenticated by the seals of the interested parties. It was then enclosed in a clay envelope and filed in the court archives.

Religion

I have already discussed the economic and social role of religion in Sumerian society, in the institution of the temple, and I have described the architecture of the temples themselves. Here we are concerned with religious beliefs and practices.

When we study the religion of ancient Mesopotamia we must realize that we are not dealing with anything comparable with Judaism, Christianity, Islam or Buddhism. Not only was Mesopotamian religion polytheistic, not monotheistic, but the regional and chronological complexities of its development give it a structure of many overlapping and interlocking layers, which the historian might well despair of ever disentangling. We must expect inconsistencies both in the philosophy of religion and in the mythology associated with it; we must expect the importance of individual gods in the pantheon to wax and wane at different times, often in accordance with the fortunes of the cities with which they were associated; and we must expect also significant changes in emphasis and tone in the interpretation of the same rituals or myths over the centuries. Here we have room only for a very brief and oversimplified account which I shall give under four main headings: the gods and the universe; ritual; personal religion and the art of divination. Mythology will be touched on here, but I shall deal with it in greater detail in the section on literature.

All the innumerable Sumerian gods and goddesses were recognized and worshipped throughout the country, but only a few were universally rated as major divinities. Moreover, each city had its own patron god; indeed, as we have seen, the city, its land, buildings and people were regarded as the property of the deity. The three most important gods in the pantheon were the sky-god Anu (associated with Uruk), the air-god Enlil (Nippur) and the water-god Enki (Eridu); the mother-goddess Ninhursag was the chief female deity. The moon-god Nanna (known as Sin by the Semitic speakers) and his son Utu, the sun-god, and daughter Inanna, the goddess of love (better known by her Semitic name Ishtar), were also very important.

The Sumerians thought of the universe as a disc (the earth) sur-mounted by a vault (heaven), the whole structure surrounded by the ocean, called *abzu* (from which incidentally comes our own word 'abyss'), which to the Sumerians was the original element out of which the universe was created. To the Sumerians the universe and everything in it, including the activities and institutions of man, was immutable. The functioning of this unchanging universe was governed by a series of divine laws known as *mes*; about one hundred of these are known—primarily from the myth known as 'Inanna and Enki: The Transfer of the Arts of Civilization from Eridu to Uruk'—and about sixty more or less understood. They include institutions such as godship and kingship, offices such as that of the priest, crafts (of scribes, smiths, leather-workers etc.), emotions (lamentation, rejoicing etc.), attributes (truth, falsehood, wisdom etc.), general concepts (strife, peace, victory), fundamental activities (sexual intercourse), as well as objects such as different types of musical instrument, each of which had its own *me*. These *mes*, which, according to the myth just mentioned, Inanna stole from Enki (Semitic name Ea), were originally brought by Enki to Eridu. A very late text by a priest at Babylon, named Berossus, written in Greek in the third century BC, describes this story (with the Enki-Ea figure appearing under the name Oannes) and concludes with the phrase '. . . since which time nothing else has been invented'. No phrase could demonstrate more clearly the ancient view of the un-changing nature of the universe.

To the ancient Mesopotamians the gods were everywhere: not as the all-powerful omnipresence of the one Christian god, but as part of the quality of all things, inanimate or living. For instance, their understanding of the nature of water incorporated the knowledge that Enki was the god of water and that any project connected with water needed his support. This attitude is alien to modern understanding. Our appreciation of the qualities of water might be scientific (when we think of its physical and chemical properties) or utilitarian (if we think in terms of supplies of drinking water or hydro-electric schemes) or aesthetic (as we view some beautiful lake or waterfall) but not supernatural. Though some people today would regard water as part of a total divine creation (the universe), they would not recognize a special divine quality of 'wateriness' distinct from the rest of god's world. But this separateness of things and qualities, each associated with its appropriate divinity, was part of the Mesopo-tamian consciousness and finds expression in the concept of the *mes*.

Sumerian views on life after death seem to have been hazy: the few documents we have on this subject give an unclear and sometimes contradictory picture. They believed in an underworld, sometimes conceived as a huge space beneath the earth, corresponding to the vault of heaven above and approached by one or more gateways situated in the city of Uruk. The underworld was ruled by the goddess Ereshkigal (Inanna's sister) and her husband Nergal. It was a gloomy place, governed by innumerable regulations, mostly of a restrictive nature. Even visitors to the underworld (and there are tales describing visits by gods and heroes) were restricted: they could not wear new clothes, be anointed with good oil, be noisy or make love. The dead were not all treated alike: one or two texts refer to a judgement of the dead by the sun-god Utu. This presumably indicates a connection between living a good life on earth and achieving some comfort or happiness after death. However, the general impression we get is that the Sumerians would not have wasted much time worrying about life after death and would certainly not have altered their behaviour in this world in order to achieve rewards in the next.

The archaeological evidence for attitudes to life after death does not accord well with the impression we get from the literature. Graves were often abundantly equipped with the deceased's possessions and in the case of the Royal Cemetery at Ur the royal dead were accompanied by a large number of sacrificed attendants, as well as elaborate and valuable grave furniture. This suggests a systematic preparation for an after-life in which the dead would require all the equipment he needed in life—an attitude prevalent in ancient Egypt, but not one that attunes well with the shadowy gloomy world of Ereshkigal and Nergal. There are two possible explanations for this discrepancy. The first is that we are dealing with attitudes that changed with the passing of time: the wealthy graves belong to the Early Dynastic period, while most of the literary references belong to the period of the Third Dynasty of Ur, by which time Sumerian ideas had been much influenced by the Semitic ideology of the Akkadian speakers, first introduced by Sargon of Agade. Alternatively, it may be that the purpose of the rich furniture of the Early Dynastic tombs was not so much a practical preparation for the after-life as a conspicuous display of the wealth and status of the deceased for the benefit of the living. Such a display finds many general parallels in the records of anthropologists.

The focal point of ritual in Mesopotamian religion was the image of the god itself. The god was considered actually present in the image, which was most commonly made of wood and elaborately clothed or plated with gold; the eyes were made of precious stones and both gold and precious stones used in the jewellery that adorned it. With a very few and unimportant exceptions, the images were always in human form: the animal or part-animal forms found in other ancient religions, such as that of Egypt, were very rare in Mesopotamia. The home of the image was of course the temple: it lived on a pedestal situated in a recessed niche in the main chamber, visible from the courtyard through the doorways of one or more ante-rooms. The image served as the focus for ritual activities within the temple; in addition it was carried in processions and ceremonies outside the sanctuary, which served to demonstrate the connection between the city and its god.

The role of the image in the temple was the counterpart of that of the king in his palace and it was served by a retinue of temple officials, just as the king was by the royal retinue. The feeding of the image was of particular significance and actual meals were served to it daily; the ultimate destination of the food from these repasts was, in theory at least, the king, though it is unclear whether the king regularly ate the god's food or only on special occasions. In addition to the god's own meals, large quantities of food from the temple's lands were distributed among the temple personnel as part of the daily ceremonial of the sanctuary.

As well as the daily ritual of prayers and sacrifices there were regular monthly feasts (on the day of the new moon and on the seventh, fifteenth and last day of each month) and additional special festivals. The most important event of the Sumerian year was the New Year holiday, which was celebrated over several days. The high point of this festival was the celebration of the Sacred Marriage between the king, representing the god, and one of the priestesses representing the goddess, which was meant to ensure the fertility and prosperity of the city, the land and the people. Texts of the period of the Third Dynasty of Ur record the marriage of Anu and Inanna at Uruk, of Nanna and Gula at Ur, of Ningursu and Baba at Lagash and of Enlil and Ninlil at Nippur.

We know very little about the functions of the personnel involved in the cult, though we know the names of many different priestly offices. The administrative head of the temple was the *sanga* while the spiritual head was the *en*, a role which was apparently sometimes filled by a woman. As well as the subsidiary priests, there were singers, musicians, eunuchs and sometimes prostitutes involved directly in cult practices in addition to a vast body of administrative and labouring personnel involved in the economic life of the temple.

It must be pointed out that the rituals described briefly here, though enacted in the interests of the whole community, were the concern of the priests and the king only. The common man did not participate in the ceremonies and to a great extent was excluded from even watching them. However, the major festivals involved processions of the image through the city streets and often to a shrine outside the walls and these processions were joyous public occasions, described by A. Leo Oppenheim as 'a collective outing of the city and its god'.

We know very little about the part religion played in the life of the private individual in Sumer, although there are texts which give us some indirect information on this subject. In strong contrast to the situation in later religions, the individual was, as we have just seen, largely excluded from cult practice; moreover his religion made few demands on him: prayers and fasting, for instance, seem to have been required only of the king. From the time of the Third Dynasty of Ur the archaeological record reveals private chapels attached to individual houses, as well as the public temples of the city, and these were presumably the scene of private worship. Such chapels did not exist in earlier periods and we do not know what form private worship took, though the discovery of small stone figures portrayed in attitudes of prayer and inscribed with personal names in excavations of temples of the Early Dynastic period suggests that the individual may have worshipped through his image, which represented him, indeed for this purpose *was* him, just as the divine image *was* the god. This, however, is speculation: we have no texts to help us interpret these figures.

As we have seen, on a social level the individual was the servant of the god in the temple to which he belonged and this relationship was crucial in the economic organization of the early Sumerian city states. However, the personal experience of the individual in coping with life was expressed in quite a different fashion. There seems to have been a concept of a personal god, whose job it was to act as an intermediary and intercede on the behalf of the individual in the assembly of the major gods. In addition, the well-being of the individual was dependent on the immediate presence of supernatural power in the form of what are usually described as 'protective spirits'. These were four in number, each with a different function. As Oppenheim has suggested, they can be regarded as the mythological expression of psychological experience, external manifestations of different aspects of the ego.

The Sumerian world was populated by demons, as well as by gods and protective spirits: these were visitors from the underworld, sometimes ghosts of the human dead. Their favourite haunts were deserts, graveyards and ruins. They were responsible for sickness and many other misfortunes and many magical devices were used against them.

Witchcraft too was prevalent and a number of texts describe exorcism and other magic rites designed to provide protection against evil, or to inflict evil on another or to cleanse the person after contact with dangerous phenomena.

Furthermore the life of the individual, as well as that of the state, was ordered to a very great degree by the reading of omens, the art of the diviner.

We have a large number of tablets referring to omens from the Old Babylonian period onwards and there is no doubt that this was a most

Small stone figures, hands clasped, found in Early Dynastic temples, suggest that the people worshipped there through an image rather than in person.

important aspect of Babylonian and Assyrian civilization. Indeed Akkadian divination was much respected all over the Near East and we find copies of omen texts in the Elamite and Hittite kingdoms where they were even translated into the Elamite and Hittite languages. We have no omen texts for the Sumerian period and the Sumerians clearly did not depend as heavily on divination for the ordering of their lives as did the Semitic speakers. We do know, however, that divination was used—specifically extispicy (the reading of animal entrails)—in the appointment of the high priest of the city god, the *en*.

Divination is a means of communication with supernatural forces which were thought to shape the history of the individual or group and were willing on occasion to divulge their intentions, either voluntarily or when asked, if approached in the correct manner. Manifestations of divine intentions which appeared without asking include the births of malformed animals or children, the behaviour of animals and, especially, dreams. The interpretation of dreams in fact formed a special branch of the diviner's art. The deliberate soliciting of divine intentions was made, in Old Babylonian times, in a number of different ways, including the observation of oil in water (lecanomancy) and the observation of smoke from incense (libanomancy). However, by far the most important methods involved the medium of the body of a slaughtered animal or bird; either only the liver was used (hepatoscopy) or all the entrails (extispicy). The concentration on the liver alone became more important with the passing of time and archaeological excavations have yielded clay models of livers, with the significance of the different parts inscribed upon them, presumably used in the training of diviners. The only practice for which we have definite evidence in the Sumerian period is extispicy.

Omens had to be consulted by the king before any act of political significance and in the later periods there were many rival diviners attached to the royal court. Divination was also widely used by the individual in the conduct of his private and business life. The diviners themselves were priests and they seem to have belonged to a professional association, which organized their training.

Literature

The earliest 'literary' works in cuneiform are fragments from the end of the Early Dynastic period, but most of the myths and fables which constituted the main part of Sumerian literature were created or written down for the first time towards the end of the third millennium BC in the time of the Third Dynasty of Ur, though very few documents of this period survive. Fortunately for us the scribes of the Old Babylonian period revered the ancient Sumerian texts and much of the work in the schools involved the copying, translation and revision of Sumerian writings as

All kinds of heroic tales were spun about Gilgamesh, king of Uruk. Popular from Predynastic times, when he was portrayed, for example, in company with a boatman (below), he is still found 7 or 8 hundred years later battling with a lion on a seal of the Akkadian period (above).

well as the creation of a new Akkadian literature. For this reason we are often able to supplement the information we have from incomplete Sumerian texts by that derived from later and better-preserved versions. These may be copies of the original texts in Sumerian, translations into Akkadian or new, Akkadian versions of the same stories. For instance the Flood story is known from only one Sumerian tablet, of which a mere third is preserved; however we can fill out the story from the rather numerous Akkadian versions of this tale. In fact the majority of the five thousand or so tablets that can be described as Sumerian 'literature' are late copies, either from the Old Babylonian period (many from the sacred library at Nippur) or from the much later royal library of Assur-banipal, the last great Assyrian king (668–627 BC) at Nineveh. This, of course, leads to a number of problems of interpretation, since we do not necessarily know whether we are dealing with an original Sumerian story, one which has been somewhat revised or a totally different story employing only the same theme. With this reservation in mind, we shall now look briefly at the main classes of Sumerian liberature: myths and epics, hymns and lamentations and 'wisdom literature' (disputations, essays and proverbs). It is worth emphasizing here the point already made that Sumerian literature was created for social purposes and does not concern, except incidentally, personal experience.

The Sumerian and Akkadian myths and epic tales are the earliest works of this kind in the world, but they appear rather late in the development of Mesopotamian civilization itself and they do not appear in a religious context, although their subject matter is often enough the world of the gods. Twenty different Sumerian myths are known to date; the main protagonists are the gods Enlil, Enki and Dumuzi and the goddess Inanna. The epics are similar in form to the myths, but have mortal heroes rather than gods as their subject matter. Nine Sumerian epic tales have been identified, of which five concern the most famous of ancient heroes, Gilgamesh, two are about the hero Enmerkar and the other two about the hero Lugulbanda. The Sumerian epics, unlike the better known Greek, Indian or Teutonic epics, consist of separate tales of varying length, not originally forming part of a larger unit (though often treated as such by modern scholars). Both the myths and epics were originally several hundred lines long and are written in the form of narrative poetry (lacking metre and rhyme, but employing other poetic devices such as static epithets, lengthy repetitions and recurrent formulas).

We do not know for what audience the myths and epics were composed. Kramer believes that a key figure in the development of Sumerian literature was the *nar*, a character sometimes mentioned in the hymns who is interpreted by Kramer as a minstrel. According to this view the epics represent a written version of a much earlier oral tradition, comparable to the Homeric epics of Greece. But one might suggest—a little harshly

One piece of Sumerian sculpture that appeals to modern taste ▶
is a bronze bust thought to portray Sargon of Agade.

perhaps—that the foundation for this view lies not in the meagre Sumerian evidence, but in the *desire* to find a parallel for the Sumerian situation in Homeric Greece. An alternative view has been expressed by Oppenheim, who believes that the epics were meant to be read, not recited, and that they were the conscious invention of 'Sumerian court poets and of the Old Babylonian scribes imitating them, bent on exploiting the artistic possibilities of a new literary language'.

Hymns were a very well developed literary form in Sumer. From fewer than fifty to nearly four hundred lines long, they extol gods or kings or the temples themselves. Related to the hymns are the lamentations, which are of two main kinds, those bewailing the destruction of Sumerian cities (the most famous one concerns the destruction of Ur by the Elamites at the end of the Third Dynasty of Ur, shortly before 2000 BC) and those lamenting the death of the god Dumuzi. It is generally assumed that both hymns and lamentations formed part of the temple cult, but it must be noted that they have been found not in the temples but in the 'library' areas of the cities and they must presumably have been composed, like the other literary works, by *edubba* personnel, by, for want of a better word, the school-teachers. It is nonetheless reasonable to accept that they were used in the temple ritual. We know that the hymns at least were sometimes accompanied by music, since Sumerian scribes themselves classified some of the hymns according to the different musical instruments that accompanied them.

In a different class from the documents already discussed is the so-called 'wisdom literature', which comprises disputations, essays and proverbs. The disputations take the form of a highly stylized debate between contrasting pairs of animals, people or objects, such as 'The Dispute between Summer and Winter' or 'The Dispute between Cattle and Grain'. The essays, by contrast, are few in number and do not seem to have a standard form. Collections of proverbs were immensely popular with the Sumerian scribes: more than a thousand proverbs are known, recorded on about seven hundred different tablets. Many of these proverbs are more or less unintelligible and must reflect attributes of Sumerian society that mean little to us. Others, however, immediately strike a chord in our own experience and I find that in these documents alone, of all the ancient Mesopotamian literature, do I feel at all close to those who wrote them—and that perhaps only because in these proverbs the Sumerian scribes have trapped some of the universal aspects of human life. Here are just a few of these undating words of wisdom from the Sumerian tablets:

'You don't tell me what you have found; you only tell me what you have lost.'

'Who has much silver may be happy; who has much grain may be glad; but he who has nothing can sleep.'

'Into an open mouth a fly enters.'

◀ *Most Sumerian statues were stone but were not usually as big as this one from Lagash of the city's governor, Gudea.*

'A cat—for its thoughts; a mongoose—for its actions.'
'A scribe who knows not Sumerian, what kind of a scribe is he?'
'For his pleasure—marriage; on thinking it over—divorce.'
'Who has not supported a wife or child has not borne a leash.'
'The traveller from distant places is an everlasting liar.'
'Friendship lasts a day; kinship lasts for ever.'
'You can have a king and you can have a lord, but the man to fear is the tax-collector.'

Music

Music was obviously of great importance in the lives of the Sumerians as we know from both documentary and archaeological sources. We have tablets that suggest that instrumental music, singing and dancing were features of popular entertainment in the public square, as well as playing a major role in the entertainment of the royal court and an integral and perhaps primary role in the daily ritual of the temple. Documents refer to a large number of different musical instruments and their importance in Sumerian life is indicated by the occurrence of several different instruments in the list of divine laws or *mes*—in other words each of these instruments was regarded as a vital, separate part of the universe. The documents unfortunately do not tell us what kind of instruments the names refer to, but the archaeological evidence can tell us some of the instruments in use, though it cannot tell us under what names they appear in the documents. Musical instruments have been found on a number of sites, but by far the best known are those from the Royal Cemetery at Ur. Two types of string instruments were found in these tombs: the harp and the lyre. Two forms of harp occur, a bow-shaped and a more rectangular variety. The number of strings ranged from four to as many as twenty-one, though seven was a common number. The largest of the Ur examples was bow-shaped, had eleven strings and was almost without any decoration at all. True lyres, with two arms, a crossbar and strings stretched over a bridge on the soundbox were also very popular. The lyres from Ur had seven, eight or eleven strings and were often elaborately decorated: on one, for instance, the sound box was surmounted by a splendid gold and lapis lazuli calf's head. Wind instruments included three-holed reed flutes, four-holed single and double pipes and curved trumpets. Percussion instruments included drums of many kinds (the largest being the temple kettle-drums, measuring up to 1·5 metres across), timbrels and sistrum. Of the nature of the music played we know nothing: neither the literature nor the archaeology can recreate lost sounds.

Both temple and palace households supported professional musicians and we may guess that 'amateur' music played an important part in every-day life. Music appears in the documents in the context of religious ritual

108

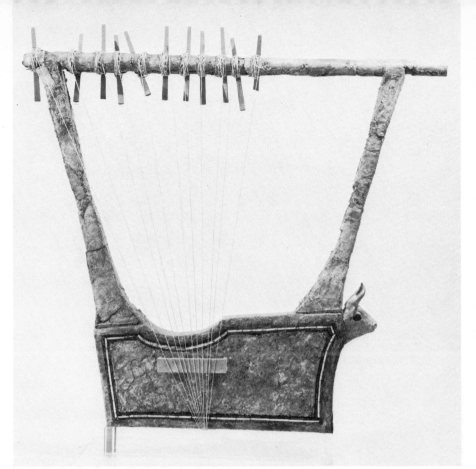

Expensively decorated musical instruments recovered from the royal tombs at Ur included a lyre bedizened in sheet silver (above reassembled and below during excavation).

on the one hand and entertainment and pleasure on the other; martial music is not mentioned in Sumerian times, though we know that at a later stage the Assyrians certainly used military trumpets.

The visual arts

Many books on the art of ancient Mesopotamia dismiss some of the finest products of Sumerian civilization, such as the objects from Ur already described, as works of high craftsmanship only, not to be classified as true 'works of art'—whatever that may mean! This is not a valid distinction to make in the Sumerian context, for, if it were carried to its logical conclusion, we should end up without any 'works of art' at all. Sumerian artists *were* craftsmen: they made objects to be used (though some of the uses were ritual rather than practical), which they produced as beautifully as their skills and the resources at their disposal allowed. That some of the results appeal to modern Western taste while others leave us cold is an accident of aesthetic history. It is interesting that, unlike the scribes and perhaps the musicians of the time, Sumerian artists were not very highly regarded. In the tablets they appear not as 'artists', but under separate headings as stone-workers, metal-workers, jewellers, seal-cutters and so on and clearly shared the same status as other craftsmen concerned with more prosaic objects, such as leather- or basket-workers. Here I shall look briefly at architecture, statuary and seal-cutting.

Elaborate architecture appears in the first instance exclusively in a religious context: until relatively late in the Early Dynastic period the temples were the only large, elaborate and decorated buildings in Mesopotamian cities. Later in Sumerian times royal palaces were also impressive buildings and the later Babylonian and Assyrian palaces were very elaborately decorated indeed, that at Babylon, with its famous lion gates, being the best known. I have already described some Sumerian temple architecture and here I shall merely reiterate two important points. The development of temple architecture was characterized by two main features: the need to raise the temple physically and symbolically above the city to which it belonged and the desire to relieve the dull flat monochrome effect which is so characteristic of mud-brick architecture. The first need led initially to the erection of platforms on which the temples were constructed and ultimately to the vast ziggurats of the period of the Third Dynasty of Ur and later. The second need led on the one hand to the widespread use of niches, recesses and buttresses which relieved the 'flat' impression and, on the other, to the use of coloured decoration, usually in red, black and white; this took a number of forms, but one of the most characteristic was in the use of clay cone mosaic.

Sumerian statuary takes the form of more or less realistic human figures, most commonly in stone. Some large statues are known, including

One of the finest pieces of Predynastic sculpture comes from Uruk and is perhaps a mask.
Carved in a fine-grained, translucent marble, it is grooved to take a wig.

a number of famous ones portraying Gudea, ruler of Lagash in about 2200 BC, but the majority of the figures from the Sumerian period are small votive statuettes found in the temples: important groups come from Tell Asmar in the Diyala area and from Mari in the far north-west as well as from the southern cities. They portray both men and women as short and thickset with thick necks, broad noses and enormous eyes. These figurines are attractive but of no great aesthetic power. By contrast one of the very few Sumerian works that *does* appeal powerfully to our own taste is the bronze head of a king of the Akkad period, often believed to be that of Sargon himself—a portrait endowed with exceptional dignity and force. We may suspect a completely lost class of wooden statuary; certainly we know that the divine images were usually made of wood and if the god himself might appear in wooden form, so surely might his worshippers.

The art of the seal-cutter is different in kind to that of the sculptor in stone or bronze and appears in a different context. It is a miniature art, involving the excision of minute but elaborate designs on small stone cylinders, which were rolled on wet clay to produce a picture in the form of a frieze. They were not associated with temple ritual or royal ceremonial, but were personal possessions, used initially perhaps as amulets, later certainly as marks of private ownership. Some of the most beautiful seals belong to the protoliterate period, when they often portrayed domestic cattle, wild deer and goats and simple ritual scenes. In the early part of the Early Dynastic period abstract designs were in favour, though representational designs reappeared later in the period, often in the form of scenes of combat between different types of animal or between animals and men. The Sargonid period saw the height of the seal-cutter's art, with elaborate mythological scenes accompanied by cuneiform inscriptions, often including the name of the owner. Seals, often of fine quality, continued to be made throughout Mesopotamian history, so that Herodotus could write of latter-day Babylonians that 'everyone owns a seal'.

Knowledge and science

In prehistoric times technological and economic progress occurred in the context of improvements in everyday practice and these improvements were presumably passed on by precept and example from father to son and master to apprentice. In the historic period with the invention of writing, it became possible, in theory at least, to build up a body of written knowledge, independent of the 'production line' on which the principles were applied. In practice this did not happen to any great extent in ancient Mesopotamia and even in late Babylonian and Assyrian times many subjects were never written down in this manner. Childe argued cogently that this arose from the division of society into classes that accompanied the development of civilization. While scribes belonged to a respected

One way in which the Sumerians could label goods, even before the invention of writing, was by affixing a strip of wet clay with some distinguishing mark stamped or rolled on to it from a stone seal (right). The seals were intricately carved, some of the most imaginative dating from the earliest periods (impression above) and abstract and highly stylized designs marking out Early Dynastic examples (impression below left). By the Akkadian period they were carrying written inscriptions too (impression below right).

higher stratum, artisans did not, so the applied science of craft lore was not regarded as a suitable subject for the scribe's art. However, some sciences and pseudo-sciences—presumably invested with high social status—*were* written down: by late Babylonian times (in the first millennium BC) we find mathematical, medical, surgical, astronomical and astrological texts, as well as the large number of texts concerned with divination, which incorporated a considerable body of accurate anatomical information. From the Sumerian period we really have very few 'scientific' texts: a small number of mathematical texts, the medical prescription tablet described earlier and the so-called 'Farmer's Almanac', which contains detailed instructions about farming practice, are the only documents to fall into this category. However it is true to say that almost all the Old Babylonian 'scientific' texts, especially the mathematical and medical ones, demonstrate a debt to earlier—Sumerian—achievement. Here I shall confine myself to a very brief note about mathematics.

As we have already seen, mathematics is represented in the documentary record by two kinds of tablets: tables and problems. Although we have tablets of both types from the Sumerian period, the vast majority of the problem tablets come from the Old Babylonian period. Scholars such as Kramer, however, argue that these are based on Sumerian prototypes, since most of the technical terms used are in the Sumerian language. This is probable, but, as we are dealing with a branch of knowledge that was not static but that developed with time, we have no way of knowing, in the absence of contemporary texts, the degree of achievement attained by Sumerian mathematicians. What *is* clear is the context in which it developed: Sumerian mathematics, as surely as writing itself, had its roots in the need to organize and record the affairs of the temple. The Sumerians and their Old Babylonian successors were interested not in pure mathematics, but in the practical problems that faced them: the quantity of seed needed to sow a field; the ration required for a particular work force; the quantities of grain needed for brewing the temple beer; or the area of land to be flooded by a given volume of water.

The earliest account tablets of the protoliterate period, from Uruk and Jamdat Nasr, employed on some occasions a decimal system of notation with D standing for 1, o for 10 and o for 100, but others used the so-called sexagesimal system with the symbols D for 1, o for 10, D for 60, O for 600. By Early Dynastic times only the sexagesimal system was used. It remained in use until the end of Babylonian civilization and indeed survives to this day in the way in which we divide the circle and the clock. The Sumerians employed positional numeration, i.e. the system of 'place value' that we ourselves use. They appear not to have mastered the principles of fractions, but had separate symbols for those most commonly needed: one half, one third and two thirds. By Old Babylonian times, however, the mathematicians handled fractional quantities with ease and complete mastery. The notational system lacked a sign for zero, a defect that was eventually corrected in the first millennium BC.

The tables of the Old Babylonian period include multiplication and division tables, tables of squares, cubes and other powers, square and cube roots and lists of figures—exponential functions—needed to calculate compound interest. Many of the problems involve the calculation of areas and volumes. These were of course needed for practical purposes and, as absolute accuracy was not necessary, approximations were often used. However a number of principles of geometry were accurately applied. The Sumerians already calculated the areas of rectangular fields correctly by multiplying the length by the breadth. Their Old Babylonian successors understood the relationship we describe as Pythagoras' theorem and they could also correctly calculate the height of an arc, given the length of its chord and the diameter of the circle. In both these achievements and several others they were in advance of Egyptian mathematicians, but their estimation of the quantity we call π, which they were generally content to take as equivalent to three, was much less accurate than that used in Egypt.

Bertrand Russell claimed that the Greeks invented mathematics and dismissed the Babylonians' work as rules of thumb. This seems unjust, for although the Babylonian mathematicians remained severely restricted by their utilitarian objectives, they did invent numerical techniques with the potential for infinite development and they did move, however tentatively, towards an understanding of some general principles. In fact, the Greeks inherited Babylonian mathematics which formed the basis of their own much higher achievement. And Babylonian mathematics itself, as we have seen, was rooted in Sumerian achievement. It was the Sumerian scribes who were the true pioneers; in Childe's words they '. . . were experimenting in an utterly strange and uncharted domain . . . the problems they had to solve were absolutely new . . . the ancient mathematicians had actually to invent methods for their solution'. Just as a child's first steps are the most difficult he ever takes, so these first steps in a totally new discipline were greater achievements than any subsequently made within it. Fumbling and unsure though they seem to us, we should be wrong to despise them.

Each square on this tablet of accounts carries a symbol for some commodity and a number. The D-shaped signs and the varying sizes of O make up the numbers.

Chapter VI   The Indus Valley

The setting

The Indus Valley or Harappan civilization, as it is often called after one of the two main sites, covered a larger area than that of either ancient Mesopotamia or Egypt, extending over a distance of some 1,600 kilometres from Rupar at the foot of the Simla hills to Sutkagen Dor near the present coast of the Arabian Sea. Moreover, from Sutkagen Dor on the Makran coast to the recently discovered sites on the west coast of India, on the eastern side of the Gulf of Cambay, is about 1,200 kilometres of seaboard. In all, Indus Valley sites have been found over a roughly triangular area covering approximately one million square kilometres of land.

The one hundred or so known sites of the Indus Valley civilization fall into two main groups (excluding the south-western extension in the Gulf of Cambay area): a northern (Punjab) group with Harappa as its main city and a southern (Sind) one with Mohenjo-Daro as its capital. Strictly speaking only the southern group is in the Indus Valley itself, since there are no sites actually on the Indus more than 250 kilometres from the sea. The northern sites lie on the tributaries of the Indus—the Ravi and the Sutlej—and especially on the former river Ghaggar which flowed south of the Sutlej until it petered out in the Bahawalpur deserts or perhaps even struggled through to the sea. Between the two groups of sites is a sterile area approximately 200 kilometres long without any known sites at all.

Today the environment of most of the area formerly covered by the Indus civilization seems hostile. The delta is a vast area of marsh and lagoons which absorb much of the water of the Indus before it debouches into the Arabian Sea through a number of small channels which are constantly changing course. The alluvial plain of Sind is arid and much of it is occupied by desert or near-desert scrub; the rather small cultivated patches are supported by extensive irrigation works. Only the Punjab is a prosperous agricultural area today and this is achieved by a combination of irrigation and natural rainfall, the latter being much higher here than in Sind. The climate is very hot, especially in the south, and, in spite of the low rainfall, humidity is high because of the proximity of the sea. So unfavourable do these conditions seem for the support of civilized life that it used to be argued that very different climatic conditions must have obtained at the time when the Indus civilization flowered. It was assumed that there must have been much more rain and a number of arguments were used to support this. The use of baked brick rather than sun-dried mud-brick and the presence of efficient drains in the Indus cities were cited as evidence of wetter conditions. The faunal evidence indicated a much more abundant vegetation than that of the present day and that, it was argued, could only have grown in conditions of greater rainfall: the remains of tigers, rhinoceroses, elephants, monkeys and other jungle creatures all appear. An additional argument for denser vegetation in Indus civilization times was the calculation of the very large amount of timber that would have been required to fire all the bricks used in the Indus cities. Today it is recognized that there must indeed have been much more woodland than today, but the hydrologists, especially R. L. Raikes, maintain that this would not have required more rainfall than at present. The Indus soils would originally have supported a strip of dense woodland on either side of the river, shading through savannah vegetation to desert scrub with distance from the river. This woodland was destroyed not by changing climatic conditions but by man (through excessive tree-felling) and by his beasts (especially grazing sheep and goats). The drains, Raikes suggests, were simply for domestic purposes and baked brick was used because it was a better building material than mud-brick, in wet or dry conditions.

So it seems we may assume a climate similar to today's for the third millennium BC. The desolate nature of the countryside today is the result of over-exploitation of an environment that must always have been difficult—a situation similar to that which we deduced for Sumer. Indeed there were several features of the Indus environment that parallel that of southern Mesopotamia and, incidentally, contrast with that of Egypt. The Indus floods, like those of the Tigris and Euphrates, are erratic and difficult to control. The southern Indus cities were very vulnerable to flooding. The excavations at Mohenjo-Daro have demonstrated that much time and effort was devoted to combating a series of very serious floods. In fact these floods were not mainly due to the annual flooding of the whole Indus system as a result of the spring snowmelt. Instead it seems that periodic uplifts of the land between Mohenjo-Daro and the coast dammed up much of the river water behind a large barrier. Certainly the flooding problem at Mohenjo-Daro was more serious than that recorded on any Mesopotamian site. It may indeed have contributed crucially to the decline and fall of the civilization. Like the Mesopotamian cities also, the Indus cities were vulnerable to changes in the course of the river. Unfortunately we know very little about the historical development of any individual Indus city or of the whole civilization, so it is difficult to assess the role played by environmental factors, including the three important ones I have mentioned: destruction of vegetation, excessive flooding and alteration in river course—in their history. It seems likely, however, that the Indus environment posed greater problems than those that faced either the ancient Egyptians or the Mesopotamians. And it seems possible, moreover, that the citizens of the Indus Valley finally succumbed to the problems of their environment, unlike the Egyptians or the Mesopotamians who survived, in spite of theirs, long after the Indus cities had foundered.

Archaeology and chronology

We cannot write a history of the Indus civilization, as we can of the successive civilizations of Mesopotamia. The Indus script is undeciphered and, even if we were able to read the inscriptions, it is unlikely that any of the existing documents would help us to reconstruct military or political history. Instead we are dependent on the archaeological record for a reconstruction of development and decline. This means that we must be content with a generalized account, lacking not only the kind of political and military outline we have for Mesopotamia, but even the names of the rulers. Moreover, even the archaeological information is extremely limited—though this can be remedied by more and better excavations in the future. At the moment we can reconstruct only the barest outline. Successive layers of former settlement revealed at the excavated sites provide us with the information for the reconstruction of the 'history'. We can then provide this historical development with some absolute dates, provided on the one hand by radiocarbon analysis and, on the other, by a number of objects manufactured in the Indus civilization area that reappear in datable deposits on Mesopotamian sites.

It has been customary to maintain that the Indus civilization appeared suddenly more or less in its mature form. This view owes more to theory than to the evidence, which is meagre. Sir Mortimer Wheeler maintains that '. . . a high measure of suddenness may still be expected in the actual genesis of the expansive metropolitan culture', although he admits almost in the same breath that 'we still know nothing of the beginning of Mohenjo-Daro and little enough of the beginning of Harappa'. In fact we know very little about anything before the mature civilization; this is because very few excavations have examined early levels of settlement on Indus sites; not because such levels do not exist. What evidence there is does not seem to me to support the idea of a very sudden development. Five sites of the Indus civilization have produced evidence of occupation earlier

Like the Mesopotamian cities, the cities of the Indus civilization flourished in fertile river valleys where abundant vegetation supported a varied wild life. Now Mohenjo-Daro looms up out of a dry landscape (top) and jungle creatures that the inhabitants once portrayed have vanished (above and right).

than the mature phase: both Mohenjo-Daro and Harappa themselves, Kalibangan, Amri and Kot Diji. The nature of the early Mohenjo-Daro occupation is unknown, but the early levels on the other four sites have produced pottery and other artefacts different from the typical Harappan repertoire. They are usually interpreted as village cultures which were replaced by the Indus civilization. However, these settlements were *not* simple agricultural villages of the type characteristic of the early farming era in western Asia: two at least—Kot Diji and Kalibangan—were fortified townships. Nor is there evidence for sudden cultural replacement: Harappan pottery types occur in small quantities in these early deposits, in association with a majority of non-Harappan wares. It seems possible that these early cultures were actually the ancestors of the Indus civilization —not something separate and different. It is true that we cannot trace the development on any of the excavated sites (the evidence from Harappa and Kalibangan is not clear; at Amri and Kot Diji the Indus elements in the early deposits do look out of place), but this does not mean that it might not have occurred elsewhere out of the same kind of background. Future excavations at Mohenjo-Daro might provide the answer to the problem. A boring drilled on this site by George Dales in 1964 near the so-called HR mound revealed, astonishingly, that there was evidence of occupation at a depth of about 12 metres below the present surface of the flood plain (about 22 metres below the top of the adjacent mound) and more recent wells drilled by Unesco have found occupation as low as 18 metres below the flood plain. This great depth may be partly occupied by flood deposits, such as are known from higher levels on this site; moreover, at present, we do not know whether the material from the early levels is of Harappan type or not. However, on any showing, the site of Mohenjo-Daro must have been occupied for a long period before the date of the main excavated occupation. I believe that, when sufficient excavation has been undertaken, we may have evidence for the local genesis of Harappan civilization as clear as that which we have for the creation of Sumerian civilization in southern Mesopotamia.

We have several radiocarbon dates for the pre-Harappan layers at Kalibangan and Kot Diji; most of them fall between about 2100 and 2470 bc, which give corrected dates in the range 3150–2800 BC. There is a date for a late Kot Dijian level of 1975 bc (*c.* 2400 BC), which is undoubtedly contemporary with the mature Harappan civilization.

The mature or developed Harappan civilization has been divided into a number of phases on individual sites, but no general sequence has been worked out for the whole civilization or even for a region, so for the moment we are obliged to treat the whole thing as one unit. We have a number of radiocarbon dates from Mohenjo-Daro, Kalibangan, Lothal and Rojdi, which fall between about 1950 and 1650 bc (*c.* 2400–2000 BC). If the corrected dates are to be trusted, they make the mature Harappan

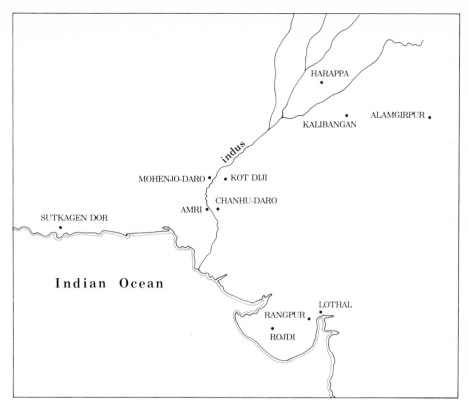

The cities of the Indus civilization were spread over an area twice the size of Meso-potamia, with distances of hundreds of kilometres between them. They formed two geographical groups separated by desert. All have been found to have been never-theless alike in plan, in design and in way of life.

civilization approximately contemporary with the Sargonid and Third Dynasty of Ur periods in Mesopotamia, while the pre-Harappan or Early Harappan period is contemporary with the Early Dynastic period of Sumer. The evidence of the Indus Valley manufactures found in Meso-potamia fits these dates well: a few come from Early Dynastic III contexts, most from the Sargonid period and a few more from deposits of the Third Dynasty of Ur and the Larsa periods (down to about 1900 BC).

The end of the Indus civilization poses a problem of some complexity, which I shall deal with in a later section. Here I am concerned only with its date. We have no radiocarbon dates (except very anomalous ones) later than about 1600 bc (*c*. 1900 BC). Moreover, no Indus imports have been identified in Mesopotamia after the end of the Larsa period. There-fore it seems likely that the fall of the civilization or the onset of its decline (depending on whether one believes it occurred suddenly or gradually) came not long after 1900 BC.

The cities

Of the hundred or more Harappan towns known, two—Harappa and Mohenjo-Daro—are immensely larger than all the others: each more than 5 kilometres in circumference, they occupy several hundred hectares of land, whereas most of the other towns cover less than 10 hectares. So great is this difference that we must regard these two cities as capitals, metropolises, with controlling political power over the other much smaller towns. It is clear that the situation was quite different from that obtaining in Mesopotamia in Early Dynastic times, where the individual city states were largely independent and, when one did temporarily gain control over the whole of Sumer, it was a case of being first among equals. In the case of the Indus civilization, it is inconceivable that the little provincial towns could ever have become state capitals: for instance, Chanhu-Daro could never have been independent of Mohenjo-Daro or Kalibangan of Harappa. The relationship between the two metropolises themselves poses an interesting problem. Although some 600 kilometres separates them, they are culturally indistinguishable, as are all the towns within the vast area occupied by the Indus civilization. Stuart Piggott and others have suggested that there was a twofold political control, with Harappa capital of the Punjab province, Mohenjo-Daro of Sind. Such a duality is plausible on geographical grounds and certainly characterized the political organization of northern India at various times in the historical period—under the Kushan, Arab and Mogul regimes. However, so inadequate is our knowledge of the chronology of the Indus civilization that we simply do not know whether the main periods of development at Mohenjo-Daro and Harappa were contemporary or not. It is not impossible that there may have been an early centre in Sind and that, as the southern sites succumbed to the disastrous floods for which we have evidence at Mohenjo-Daro and other sites, the political centre shifted northwards to the Punjab, with its capital at Harappa. However, such chronological evidence as we do have does *not* indicate any difference between the areas. Unfortunately we do not have any radiocarbon dates from Harappa itself, but the range of dates from another northern site—Kalibangan—is closely comparable with that from Mohenjo-Daro in the south. It seems more likely to me that the two capitals flourished more or less contemporaneously.

The excavated Indus towns, the capitals and the smaller centres, share a number of features. In the first place they were laid out on a regular grid of criss-crossing straight streets—in strong contrast to the 'organic' development of Mesopotamian cities and they were possibly the earliest examples of town planning in the world. Secondly, Indus towns consist characteristically of a lower town, overlooked by a fortified citadel, usually rhomboidal in shape and situated to the west of the rest of the town: so far this arrangement has been recorded at Mohenjo-Daro, Harappa, Kalibangan and Sutkagen Dor. The lower towns were probably

The side-streets of Mohenjo-Daro were straight and narrow, closely overhung by the windowless, baked-brick walls of the houses. ▶

usually fortified also: certainly that at Kalibangan was and so, probably, was Mohenjo-Daro. Whether Harappa also had a town wall is unknown. At Lothal the whole settlement, including the citadel, was surrounded by one wall. Other characteristics of the Indus towns are the general use of baked brick and a highly organized drainage system; both these features contrast with Mesopotamian custom. I shall now consider separately the features of the capital cities and of the smaller towns.

The twin capitals of the Indus civilization were the largest cities of the ancient world, rivalled only by the Sumerian city of Uruk, which enclosed 450 hectares within its walls during the Early Dynastic period. Of the two sites, Harappa was devastated during the last century by the extraction of bricks which were used as ballast for the railway as well as for house building. However, enough remains to indicate that the layout of the city was very similar to that of Mohenjo-Daro, which is much better understood. Both sites consist of two groups of mounds: a small high one to the north-west covering the remains of the ancient citadel and a lower, more extensive group to the south-east representing the ruins of the lower town. On both sites the citadel was a parallelogram, aligned more or less north–south, measuring approximately 400×200 metres and rising about 12 metres above the flood plain. Both citadels were built on artificial platforms made of mud-brick and mud and were massively defended. At Harappa there was a wall about 14 metres wide at the base, but tapering upwards; it was mostly made of mud-brick but had an external retaining wall of baked brick. There were rectangular salients or bastions at intervals along the wall. The still unexplored main entrance was on the northern side. At Mohenjo-Daro systematic fortifications, consisting of a series of solid baked brick towers, have been excavated only in the south-east corner of the citadel, though traces of defences have been found on the western side also.

We know virtually nothing of the buildings on the citadel at Harappa, though it is clear from the excavation reports that it was densely built over. At Mohenjo-Daro, however, a number of important structures have been excavated on the citadel and we might guess that the layout was similar to Harappa.

The most important excavated buildings on the Mohenjo-Daro citadel are the Great Bath, the Granary and the so-called 'College' and 'Assembly Hall' buildings. The Great Bath measured approximately 12×7 metres and was approximately 2·5 metres deep. It was surrounded by enclosing verandas behind which, on three sides, were ranges of rooms. Across a lane to the north was a block of eight small private bathrooms arranged in two rows on either side of a passage with a drain running along it. It is a reasonable guess that the whole complex was connected with the religious life of the city: ritual ablutions are a conspicuous feature of modern Hinduism, as well as of other religions such as Islam.

◀ A terra cotta figurine from Mohenjo-Daro.

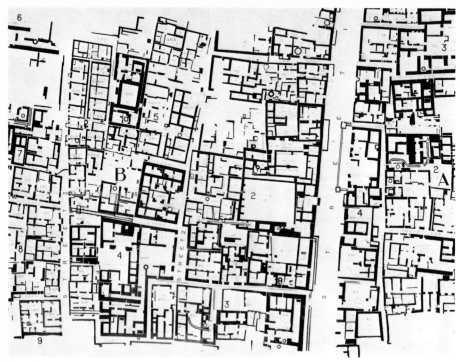

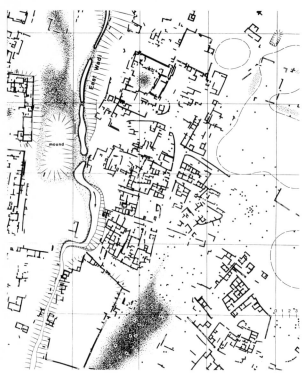

In the Indus cities public buildings were grouped on a citadel to one side of a lower town whose grid plan appears to have been laid out from the beginning (*Mohenjo-Daro* above) and contrasts with the apparently haphazard growth of Mesopotamian cities (*Tell Taya* left). Eleven blocks in the town at Mohenjo-Daro made up, with the citadel, a square city fully 1,600 metres across.

Immediately to the west of the Great Bath was the Granary. The excavated remains consist of solid blocks of brickwork divided by narrow passages, originally covering an area of approximately 46×23 metres but enlarged at an early stage by the addition of an extension of the south side. This surviving part is a podium which originally supported a timber superstructure; the criss-cross layout of passages between the blocks ensured the circulation of air beneath the Granary proper. The external walls of the podium sloped inwards and the structure was bonded and laced with timbers (as was the earliest of the towers in the south-eastern area of the citadel). The decay of these timbers had led to local collapses and subsequent patching of the brickwork. We do not know whether the citadel at Harappa enclosed a similar granary, but a group of twelve small granaries built in a similar way has been found at Harappa in the area north of the citadel, between it and the river. They each measure about $15 \cdot 6 \times 6$ metres and are arranged symmetrically in two rows on either side of a central passage. The combined floor space of the twelve granaries is close to that of the earliest phase of the large Mohenjo-Daro granary. In the same area at Harappa were at least eighteen circular brick platforms which probably surrounded mortars used for the pounding of grain with long wooden pestles, of the kind still in use in some parts of India today. There were also in this area two lines of small oblong dwellings which may have housed workmen. The whole area seems to have been given over to the preparation and storage of grain and to the accommodation of those who worked on it. It is clear that both here and at Mohenjo-Daro we are dealing with state granaries, which housed the collective product of the city's fields. We must remember that in an economy that was moneyless, but nonetheless had to deal with transactions on a state scale, the state granary must have been in some ways equivalent to the Treasury in a modern state. This must have been true of Mesopotamia also and we know from documents of the Third Dynasty of Ur period that granaries existed, some at least attached to temples. However, no granaries have been recognized among the excavated buildings of Mesopotamia and their presence must have been less dominant than those of the Indus Valley.

Returning to the citadel of Mohenjo-Daro, to the north-east of the Great Bath was the so-called 'College' building. Unfortunately we know little of its architectural history and nothing of its function, although it was identified by its excavator as 'the residence of a very high official, possibly the high priest himself, or perhaps a college of priests'. The 'Assembly Hall' is situated in the southern part of the citadel. In its original form it was a hall about 28 metres square divided into five aisles by four rows of five brick piers. It was subsequently modified several times. The interpretation of this building as a place of assembly seems reasonable.

Much of the Mohenjo-Daro citadel mound has been eroded; moreover, we do not know what kind of structure underlies the much later

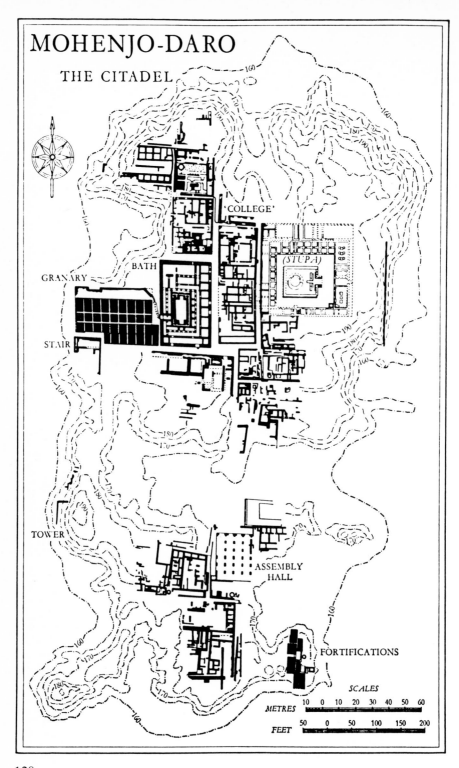

MOHENJO-DARO

THE CITADEL

COLLEGE

(STUPA)

BATH

GRANARY

STAIR

TOWER

ASSEMBLY HALL

FORTIFICATIONS

SCALES

METRES 10 0 10 20 30 40 50 60

FEET 50 0 50 100 150 200

Public buildings on the citadel at Mohenjo-Daro (*left*) have been identified as a Granary, a Bath, a 'College' and an 'Assembly Hall'. All were probably connected with the city's religious life, the Great Bath (*right* and *above*) being the scene of ritual ablutions.

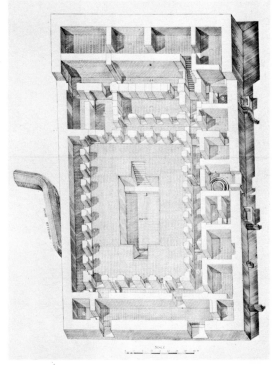

Buddhist stupa and monastery to the east of the 'College' building. The most conspicuously missing building is a temple. No temple has yet been identified with certainty on any Indus site, although one or two buildings in the lower city at Mohenjo-Daro have been described as shrines.

The lower city at Harappa has produced no intelligible plans. By contrast the basic town plan of Mohenjo-Daro is well understood. It was built on a gridiron plan of main streets running approximately north–south and east–west, dividing the area into rectangular blocks measuring about 250×370 metres. Parts of seven blocks have been excavated so far and there may originally have been twelve, with the citadel mound situated in the central western block. The main streets were up to 10 metres wide, while the lanes which subdivide the blocks range from 1·5 to 3 metres in width. The streets were unpaved but were supplied with brick drains, and brick-built manholes at intervals allowed regular clearing of the accumulation. Waste was discharged from the houses into the drains through earthenware pipes and purpose-built chutes. There were many wells in the city: some in individual houses; others, presumably public, were accessible from the streets.

A high proportion of the buildings appear to be commodious middle class houses. As houses in Asia generally are, they were centred on a courtyard on to which opened ranges of rooms. The external doors opened on to the side lanes rather than the main streets; windows were rare. Most houses had a well room with adjoining bathroom and drains led out under the floors to the street drain outside. Some houses had latrines with proper seats. The buildings were generally two storeys high originally, though none now survive above ground-floor ceiling level. A number of buildings have been excavated that were probably not for domestic use, but identification of their function is uncertain. They have approximately the same layout as the houses, with a central courtyard surrounded by rooms of various sorts, but they are sometimes larger in size and have unusual features. Some appear to have been commercial or industrial in function, whereas others look like public buildings of some sort. Some have been identified tentatively as temples or shrines, but the evidence seems meagre. Other buildings look like barracks and may have housed slaves or semi-slave labourers. The walls of the buildings were made of baked brick, but mud-brick was sometimes used internally. Surviving traces show that, sometimes at least, the walls were coated with mud plaster on the inside. Timber may have been used in the upper storeys, but evidence is lacking.

Two important features were noted at Mohenjo-Daro by all the archaeologists who have excavated there. Firstly, the city had been engulfed by extensive floods on at least three occasions. Secondly, in the later phase of the city's life both town planning and the quality of building deteriorated; slum-like subdivisions occurred in many areas.

130

Apart from Harappa and Mohenjo-Daro themselves, the only Indus civilization towns to have been investigated seriously are Kalibangan in northern Rajasthan, Chanhu-Daro south of Mohenjo-Daro and Lothal in Kathiawad. The Harappan period site at Kalibangan which, as we have seen, overlaid an earlier fortified settlement, consisted of a citadel and a lower town, both defended, and laid out, as in the two capital cities, with the citadel to the west of the main town. At Kalibangan the rhomboidal fortifications of the lower town measured rather less than 250 × 400 metres, enclosing an area of approximately ten hectares. The fortified citadel covered an area of about $1\frac{1}{2}$ hectares, to which was later added a residential annexe of approximately the same size, also defended, on the northern side. The lower town was laid out on a grid plan like all the other known Harappan towns, but for reasons which are not readily understood the alignment of the street plan is different from that of the fortifications.

Much less is known about the nature of the town at Chanhu-Daro; we do not know, for instance, whether it was ever fortified, but it seems to have been laid out on the usual grid plan and typical well-built Harappan drains ran along the streets. Two particularly interesting features were revealed by the excavations at Chanhu-Daro. One was the fact that, as at Mohenjo-Daro, the town had been inundated by floods: there was evidence that the town had been twice destroyed and rebuilt on a new plan. The second feature is that the town had been reoccupied after it had been deserted by the Harappa people, by a group described as the Jhukar culture (named after another site in Sind). This reoccupation was not urban in character and, clearly, urban life had broken down by this stage.

The excavations at Lothal have yielded information as interesting as any we have on the Indus civilization. Here in Kathiawad, where before the 1950s no site of the Indus civilization had been even suspected, has been excavated what was clearly one of the major Harappan ports. The importance of this becomes clear when we realize that the Indus civilization depended largely on trade for its existence, though probably not to the same extent as its Mesopotamian counterpart. The town of Lothal originally covered an area of about 12 hectares which was surrounded by a defensive wall; however, it expanded outside this perimeter wall and at the height of its prosperity occupied an area of about 24 or 25 hectares in all. It had the characteristic Harappan gridiron street plan and drainage system. It also had a fortified acropolis built, like the citadels of the capital cities, on an artificial platform of mud and mud-brick, but unlike those of other Harappan towns, enclosed within the main town. A mud-brick structure is probably the base of a granary, like that on the citadel at Mohenjo-Daro. However, the most interesting structure at Lothal is a large rectangular enclosure on one side of the mound, measuring about 225 × 37 metres and faced with baked brick. It had a sluice gate at one end and is interpreted as a dock used for ships sailing up the Gulf of Cambay. No such port installations have been excavated on any Mesopotamian site.

Society and people

In the absence of written documents we are woefully ignorant of the nature of Harappan society. What *is* clear is that we are dealing with an authoritarian and a hierarchical social and political system: without such a system the cultural unity found in Harappan towns from one end of the vast area occupied by the civilization to the other would be inexplicable. Likewise the planned layout of the towns, the efficient drainage systems and the existence of central 'state' granaries speak powerfully for the existence of a central authority with absolute control. What we do not know is the basis of this authority. Were the Indus cities ruled by priests deputizing for gods as in Predynastic Sumer or by mortal kings as in Mesopotamia from the Early Dynastic period onwards or perhaps by monarchs who were both kings and gods as in Egypt? We do not know: neither unequivocal temples nor recognizable palaces have yet been found in any Indus city; no royal tombs like those of Egypt or Mesopotamia have come to light. In other words, we have not excavated either the dwellings or the offices of the Indus rulers; we have not found their burial places or their bodies; we have not found a single object which we know to be one of their possessions; we do not know their names or any of their exploits. They remain shadowy figures; only the cities themselves survive as testimony to the reality and extent of their authority.

As for the rest of society, the number of substantial well-built houses at Mohenjo-Daro suggests the existence of a prosperous middle class, at least during the period of the mature civilization. And the existence of barrack-like buildings both at Harappa (in the area between the citadel and the river) and at Mohenjo-Daro (in the lower city), which are sometimes compared to recent 'coolie-lines', suggests the presence of at least a small, slave, or near-slave, working population. In addition we may assume the existence of a large body of agricultural workers, whose status would presumably have been between that of the slaves and that of the middle class. Beyond this we cannot go. We do not know whether there was an aristocracy as well as the ruling kings or priests; we do not know the status of merchants, craftsmen or the military who built and manned the defences. We do not know to what degree this was a state economy and to what, if any, extent private enterprise existed. Further excavations with a few lucky finds might help us to answer some of these questions; the decipherment of the Indus script would undoubtedly help. However it seems unlikely that we shall ever have about the Indus civilization a fraction of the information we have about its contemporaries in Egypt and Mesopotamia and there will probably remain many areas shrouded in mystery.

132

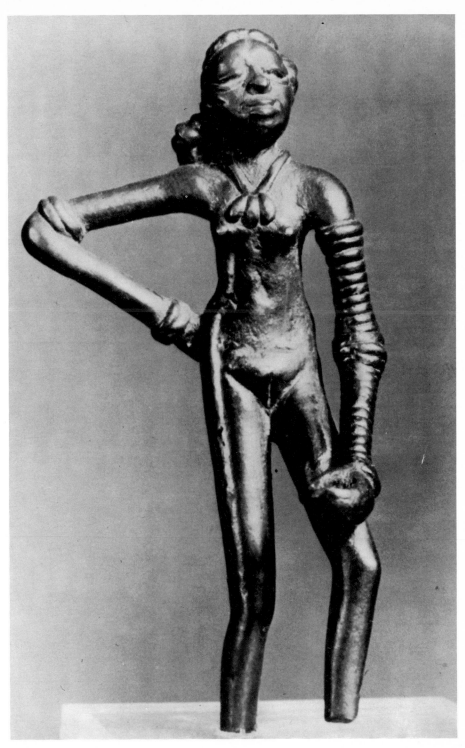

This little bronze dancing girl was found in the foundations of a house in the town at Mohenjo-Daro.

A study of the skeletons found on Harappan sites shows that the Indus population was physically diverse and almost certainly of mixed stock. Among the inhabitants of Mohenjo-Daro who were killed during the final attack on the city (of which more later) was one who was unmistakably Mongolian, perhaps from central Aisia or still further east. If the statuettes found on Harappan sites can be taken as reasonably realistic portraits, the Harappan men grew beards but not moustaches and wore their hair in a bun; they wore robes which exposed their right shoulders. The women appear to have worn short skirts with ornamental belts and elaborate jewellery and head-dresses.

Subsistence economy

As in Mesopotamia, the civilization of the Indus Valley was based on cereal agriculture, with high yields produced through irrigating the alluvial soils which retained their fertility by the deposition of silt by flood water. However, whereas in Mesopotamia traces of many irrigation works survive, in the Indus plain the alluvial deposits which have built up over the last four thousand years have totally obscured the remains of any ancient dykes, canals or field systems that may have existed. Nor, of course, do we have documents referring to irrigation works as we do for Mesopotamia. Only the knowledge that it would have been impossible to cultivate without irrigation in such an arid climate makes it certain that irrigation agriculture was the basis of the Indus civilization's prosperity, like that of its contemporaries in Mesopotamia and Egypt.

We know from surviving plant remains from the excavations that two kinds of wheat and barley were grown, though we do not know whether wheat or barley was the more important crop. In addition, rice seems to have been cultivated on the west coast of India: it has been recorded at Lothal and Rangpur. Peas, melons, dates, sesame and mustard were also cultivated, the last two probably for their oil. Cotton cloth has been found at Mohenjo-Daro and Lothal: this is the earliest evidence for the cultivation of cotton anywhere in the world.

The Indus farmers kept two varieties of domestic cattle, the humped zebu form and another, humpless form; they also bred buffalo and perhaps pigs and sheep. Camels, horses and asses were all used for transport and the elephant may have been domesticated too (pictures of elephants in association with man-made objects occur on seals, suggesting that they were domesticated or at least exploited). Both dogs and cats were kept.

Wild food resources were certainly exploited, but we have no way of estimating their importance in the diet or the economy. Fish were netted or caught by hook and line (we have evidence for both techniques) and a number of animals were hunted, including elephants, tigers, rhinoceroses, buffalo, bears, antelopes and varieties of deer.

134

Technology and crafts

The fundamental technological achievements which we discussed in connection with Sumerian civilization were also known to the Harappans. At least, we have no certain evidence that wind power was used, but it is assumed that they had sailing boats. Certainly they harnessed animals to pull carts and they used the wheel, both for transport and for making pottery; metallurgy was also known.

The industries practised in the Indus Valley were similar to those of Egypt and Mesopotamia, though there were differences in technical competence and of course in style in the different areas. Metal smiths worked in copper, gold, silver and lead. Copper smiths used pure copper, a copper-arsenic alloy or true tin bronze, but their products were of poorer quality and more primitive type than those current in Mesopotamia. They mastered *cire perdue* casting, and rivetting, but not brazing or soldering; nor did they ever produce tools with shaft-holes, as the Sumerians did. They made attractive vessels of beaten metal and the jewellers produced many types of metal beads; unlike Sumerian jewellers, however, they did not do filigree work. As well as gold, silver and copper, beads were made of faience, ground steatite paste, shell and a variety of semi-precious stones, including agate and carnelian, and a few of lapis lazuli. Particularly attractive are the etched carnelian beads: the pattern was drawn on the stone with an alkali solution (usually soda) and the stone was then heated until the alkali entered into it, making a permanent white design; alternatively the whole stone was flooded with alkali to produce a white surface which was then decorated with a black pattern, probably drawn with a solution of copper nitrate. A beadmaker's workshop was excavated at Chanhu-Daro, where evidence was found for the processes of sawing, flaking, grinding and boring of stone beads. The boring was done either with tubular bronze drills or with stone (chert) drills made with tiny cupped points to hold the abrasive and water that were used in the drilling process. Stone bracelets, rings, dice and gaming pieces were also made and also the stone seals which Sir Mortimer Wheeler has described as 'the outstanding contribution of the Indus civilization to ancient craftsmanship'. Several thousand of these seals have been excavated on Harappan sites; most of them were made of steatite and the normal shape was square with a perforated boss on the back for handling and suspension; some round examples, both with and without bosses are known, as are a few cylinder seals. The stone was first cut with a saw and finished with a knife and an abrasive; the design was cut with a small chisel and a drill and finally the whole stone was coated with an alkali and heated to produce a lustrous white surface. The designs are usually attractive and sometimes very fine indeed; they will be discussed in the section on the arts. The Indus Valley potters were also skilled craftsmen; the fast wheel was in general use and painted wares, some of very fine quality, were common. Among the crafts lost to us because they employed perishable materials were, we may guess, woodwork (certainly carpentry and woodcarving were important achievements of later Indian societies) and textile manufacture (and we know that woven cotton cloth was manufactured). Of these and other products we might suspect were made of perishable materials we have no surviving remains.

Trade

The Indus civilization was less dependent on trade for the acquisition of essential raw materials than was that of Mesopotamia. Trade was nonetheless both well organized and far-ranging. Metal ores were available within or close to the territory of the Indus civilization itself in Baluchistan (copper) and Rajasthan (copper, lead, silver). More copper and gold may have come from Afghanistan, as did probably tin and certainly the small quantities of lapis lazuli found in Indus cities. From southern India came perhaps gold and lead and certainly the much-prized sank shells. The turquoise used occasionally for beads at Mohenjo-Daro probably came from north-eastern Iran; jade either from central Asia or from China or Burma.

We know both from Indus Valley exports in Mesopotamia and from the Mesopotamian documents that there was an active trade between the Indus area and Sumer. As we have already seen Indus Valley stamp seals, etched carnelian beads, bone inlays and possibly a few other objects of Indus manufacture occur on Mesopotamian sites in contexts dating from Early Dynastic III to the end of the Larsa period (before 2400 to *c.* 1900 BC). However, it is very noticeable that there are virtually no Mesopotamian objects in the Indus Valley and very few traces of Mesopotamian influence. Two amulets of the so-called 'gatepost' type from Mohenjo-Daro look typically Mesopotamian and are probably actual imports. Apart from this, the occasional use of cylinder seals in the Indus area (in contrast to the usual square or round stamp seals) probably represents Mesopotamian influence, though the designs they bear are of Indus character, not Sumerian. Conversely, certain scenes on seals of typically Indus shape reflect Sumerian designs: for instance, one seal from Mohenjo-Daro shows a human figure holding back two rearing tigers and is often compared to similar Sumerian scenes depicting Gilgamesh between lions. We may assume that the Indus Valley cities received from Sumer some of the perishable goods that we know from the documents were exported: barley, vegetable oils and textiles seem to have been the most important. However, the traces of Mesopotamian influence in the Indus area are so rare that we can rule out the idea of Mesopotamian trading communities in the Indus Valley: there can have been nothing like the Assyrian colony at Kultepe in Anatolia at a slightly later date. Trade between the Indus civilization and Mesopotamia was certainly indirect. Equally certainly it was largely maritime in nature, along the Makran coast and up the Persian Gulf; this trade route is documented in part both by archaeological evidence and by the ancient tablets.

The Mesopotamian tablets refer to three places that are relevant to trade in the Persian Gulf and the Indian Ocean: Dilmun, Magan and Meluhha. Dilmun is plausibly identified with the island of Bahrain and adjacent areas; Magan is some area at the Indian Ocean end of the Persian Gulf (perhaps Trucial Oman on the south side or Baluchistan on the other, or indeed both areas), while Meluhha most probably refers to the Indus area itself. The documents indicate that Sumerian merchants were setting out for Dilmun as early as Early Dynastic III times (mid-third millennium BC) and for Magan in the Third Dynasty of Ur period (c. 2100–2000 BC). Direct journeys to Meluhha are not recorded, though Meluhhan ships are described in south Mesopotamian harbours, the first references appearing in the Sargonid period, indeed in a document of Sargon himself (2371–2316 BC). Archaeological evidence for the trade between Sumer and the Indus civilization in the intermediate area is meagre. Excavations on the islands of Failaka and Bahrain in the Persian Gulf have yielded circular stamp seals of a type labelled 'Persian Gulf seals', clearly related to the normal Indus seals and, in the words of Sir Mortimer Wheeler, 'made largely in and around the Persian Gulf for use in connection with long-range Indus trade'. A few actual imports from the Indus area also occur: a gaming piece and a pendant both of lapis lazuli and a stone weight from Bahrain and an etched carnelian bead from the site of Umm an-Nar in Trucial Oman. These Persian Gulf sites will be discussed further in the next chapter.

The Indus cities were also trading overland with Susa and this route may have extended to Mesopotamia itself. Several Indus objects have been found at Susa: shell and terracotta gaming pieces and the characteristic etched carnelian beads. In addition one or two objects from the Indus port site of Lothal have been claimed as imports from Susa. The only Indus find from anywhere along the route to Susa is one from the site of Tepe Yahya, south of Kerman in southern Iran, where from a level contemporary with Early Dynastic Sumer came a potsherd bearing a seal impression with unmistakable Indus signs.

As a minor aspect of Indus civilization trade, I must mention here the weights which occur in large numbers on Harappan sites. They are made of a variety of stones (chert, limestone, gneiss, steatite, slate, chalcedony, schist and hornblende have all been identified) and are finely made. A few unfinished examples indicate local manufacture. They range from jewellers' minute weights to large examples that had to be lifted by a rope or metal ring. They are most commonly cubes, though other shapes also occur, and they fall into a well defined system which is different from that

The majority of the great number of terra cotta models that have been found on the sites of Indus Valley cities are animals. The buffalo (above) has a swaying head, an ox from Mohenjo-Daro (below) is more skilfully made than most and the ram (left) is a rarity. Cows were never represented.

138

of Mesopotamia. They appear to be extremely accurate and this is in accordance with the highly disciplined nature of the Indus civilization.

Writing

The Indus script is undeciphered. Several attempts to decipher it have been published, but none has been generally accepted as valid.

Indus inscriptions have been found on stone seals and on seal impressions (on baked clay tablets), on small copper tablets, on pottery stamps and as graffiti scratched on potsherds. The majority of the inscriptions are very short with only six or so signs; the longest has only seventeen. It is possible that most of them are proper names: this would certainly be the simplest explanation of the inscriptions on seals.

The script is apparently unrelated to any other ancient script. The symbols are 'hieroglyphic' and apparently remained unchanged for the several centuries during which the script was used: no stylized form evolved, like the Egyptian hieratic or Mesopotamian cuneiform. 396 symbols have been identified, which indicates clearly that the script was not alphabetic. It was probably syllabic with the addition of some ideograms, perhaps used as determinatives as in Mesopotamia. The inscriptions begin from the right, but where there is a second line this begins from the left— an arrangement known as *boustrophedon*. An interesting feature is that accents are added to a large number of signs, suggesting a rather developed phonetic system.

We have no ancestry for the Indus script at present. Maybe when the lower levels at Harappa and Mohenjo-Daro are excavated they will provide us with finds that show us the early phases of development of this script, just as finds from Predynastic levels at Kish, Uruk and Jamdat Nasr showed us the early phases of Sumerian writing.

Religion

As we have seen, there are no excavated Indus buildings that have been identified with any degree of confidence as temples. Nor, of course, do we have any comprehensible written documents about religion (or anything else). We have therefore very little evidence about the religious life of the Indus Valley population; all we can do is pick up a few hints from motifs that figure in their art.

There are many terracotta figurines of an almost nude woman, usually interpreted as a 'Mother Goddess'. Other figurines, also of terracotta, portray pregnant women or women with children; all may indicate some kind of fertility cult. Another, related, element of Indus cult practice seems to have been phallus worship: certain polished stones, mostly small but up to about 70 centimetres in height, do seem to represent phalli, while other pierced stones are interpreted less certainly as vulva symbols. These recall the *linga* and *yoni* of Hindu cult and may represent a pre-Aryan element which survived into the so-called Aryan culture of the period after the collapse of the Indus civilization.

The most striking example of an element appearing in a Harappan context that forcibly recalls later Indian religious art occurs on three seals from Mohenjo-Daro. These depict a figure seated either on the ground or on a low stool; on two seals the head has three faces and on all it wears a horned headdress; on a single seal the figure is attended by an elephant, a tiger, a rhinoceros, a buffalo and two antelopes or goats. This figure is seen as a prototype of the Hindu Siva in his role as Pasupati, Lord of Beasts.

Moreover, the importance of water in the religious life of the Indus civilization seems certain: what Wheeler has described as 'the almost extravagant provision for bathing and drainage throughout the city' may indicate nothing more than extreme concern with domestic hygiene, but the Great Bath on the citadel of Mohenjo-Daro is more likely to have served for ritual ablutions. This is yet another feature which is characteristic of India during the historic period. Indeed what evidence we have for Indus civilization religion suggests that in this sphere at least there was some definite continuity from the Harappan period into historic times.

We cannot learn much about the Indus civilization's attitude to life after death from its burial practices. No royal burials like those of Egypt or Mesopotamia have been found; indeed only one cemetery of the Harappan period has been excavated, the so-called R37 cemetery at Harappa itself. Here fifty-seven Indus citizens were buried individually, with bodies extended north–south. With each of them were buried numbers of pottery vessels (from fifteen to forty), personal ornaments and, with some of them, toilet articles. These graves may indicate that the Indus citizens believed in an after-life in which they would need their personal possessions —as have many societies past and present (or recent). However, this may be far too simple an explanation, as may the interpretation of the symbols described in the preceding paragraphs. Religious symbolism is usually complex and many-layered and archaeologists can do little more than guess at its significance; in the case of the Indus civilization we have singularly few pointers to help us even with our guesswork.

The arts

With the exception of the stone seals, the surviving art of the Indus civilization is unimpressive and appeals little to our aesthetic taste. It is frequently suggested that there may have been a highly developed art of woodcarving, as there was in later India, but this is purely speculative: we have no surviving carved wooden objects.

Impressions from the stamp seals that Indus Valley craftsmen turned out by the hundred but to a consistently high standard. ▶

We have large numbers of terracotta figurines from Harappan sites. A few are worked with some skill and sensitivity, but most are very crudely modelled. The figurines portray both humans and animals. Among the human figures, the nearly nude women already mentioned are most common. Among the animals, cattle of different sorts are most common, but dogs, sheep and various wild animals are also depicted. In addition there are a number of small terracotta models of carts with solid wheels. Faience too was used to manufacture tiny animal figurines (sheep, dogs, monkeys and squirrels) and some of these are of fine quality.

There are a small number of human figures made of stone and bronze from Indus sites and among these are the few pieces that appeal to our own taste, such as the steatite bust of the so-called 'priest king' and the small bronze dancing girl from Mohenjo-Daro.

However it was in the art of the seal-cutter that the Indus civilization excelled. Literally thousands of Indus seals have been found; these vary considerably in quality, but as Sir Mortimer Wheeler has put it 'their average attainment is exceedingly high for what must have been an almost mass produced commodity'. The majority of the seals bear animal designs, almost always associated with an inscription; there are, however, some seals with inscriptions only, some with human or semi-human forms and some with geometric designs. The animal that occurs most commonly is an ox-like creature with only one horn, which has therefore been labelled the 'unicorn'. It is always shown with a strange object described as a 'standard' or 'manger'; it looks rather like a tablelamp set on a small one-legged table and its function is entirely unknown. Short-horned and zebu (humped) cattle are also depicted on seals, as are rhinoceroses, tigers, elephants, antelopes and crocodiles. Where the figures are meant to represent real animals, they are usually naturalistically and accurately portrayed, the best 'little masterpieces of controlled realism'—the words are again Wheeler's. Both animals and humans are shown in what appear to be religious scenes, and this religious aspect is even more apparent in the mythological animals and human-animal figures. The predominance of the 'unicorn' figure fits into this context; it is presumably not a real animal, unless two horns are in fact meant, one behind the other (but this is unlikely as two horns are always shown on other animals). Certainly fabulous are a number of composite animals: the most common form has a human face, an elephant's trunk and tusks, a bull's horns, the forepart of a ram and the hindpart of a tiger. The human-animal mixture occurs in various other forms too, including a human-faced goat and a bull-man mixture (not unlike the Cretan minotaur).

In some way related to the seals are small copper tablets which usually carry inscriptions on one side and animal figures on the other. The animal forms are drawn in outline and filled with cuprous oxide which shows red.

◀ *Among the few stone sculptures from the Indus Valley is the bust of the so-called priest-king from Mohenjo-Daro.*

The end of the Indus civilization

Some time in the early part of the second millennium BC the Indus civilization came to an end. We do not know whether this happened cataclysmically or whether urban life petered out over a period of some centuries. We do not know whether the end was more or less contemporaneous over the whole area occupied by the civilization or whether there were major regional differences. What we do know is that the civilization did end completely and was replaced by inferior, non-urban, 'squatter' cultures. Indeed all knowledge of the civilization was lost (with the possible exception of the faint memories recorded in the Rig-Veda) and was only rediscovered with the excavations at Harappa and Mohenjo-Daro in the 1920s. We have no excavated deposit of the Indus civilization that can be dated later than about 1900 BC (c. 1600 bc), but of course this does not mean that no sites survived later than this date. When we bear in mind that fewer than one tenth of all the known Indus sites have been excavated in even the most superficial fashion, we realize that we do not have the evidence at present to resolve these points.

We do not know, either, the cause or causes of the civilization's decline. Many theories have been propounded and we cannot do more here than consider the main ones. They fall into two chief categories: those that attribute the collapse to environmental factors and those that involve its deliberate destruction by warlike invaders.

That there were environmental pressures on the Indus cities is indisputable. We have seen that there is some evidence for man himself having altered his environment, for the worse, by the destruction of vegetation and perhaps by over-cultivation and over-grazing of land. Much more definite evidence makes it clear that the cities of Sind (certainly Mohenjo-Daro and Chanhu-Daro) were on several occasions inundated by serious and prolonged flooding which necessitated massive rebuilding. When we add to this the fact that at Mohenjo-Daro the latest levels indicate a progressive degeneration in the quality of building, in town planning and the standards of civil maintenance, it is possible to see, as some scholars have, the civilization dying on its feet as it gradually succumbed to environmental pressures. This answer looks relatively convincing for Mohenjo-Daro itself and perhaps for all the Sind sites. It is considerably less convincing for the sites of the Harappan province. Here there is no evidence of excessive flooding and the other environmental pressures that affected the inhabitants of Sind would also have been less pressing or absent altogether in the Punjab, with its higher rainfall and more plentiful natural vegetation. Indeed it is sometimes suggested that the main development in the Harappan area was later than that in the Mohenjo-Daro province and that Harappa assumed the leadership of the whole civilization as Mohenjo-Daro declined. We have insufficient chronological evidence either to support or to refute this (though what radiocarbon dates we do have from the northern province, from Kalibangan, suggest that this site at least was contemporary with, not later than, the southern sites). Moreover, this explanation fails to provide us with a reason for the collapse of the civilization in this area, which undoubtedly occurred at some stage, whether at the same time as, or later than in Sind province.

The other main theory holds that the Indus cities were destroyed by an invading population, often identified—perhaps too easily—with the Vedic Aryans. The only site that has produced plausible (though by no means conclusive) evidence for a final massacre is Mohenjo-Daro itself. In several areas of the city groups of skeletons were found in the latest layers, lying in houses and in streets; they included men, women and children and some showed indisputable evidence that they had been murdered. The bodies had either been hastily covered or, in most cases, not buried at all. As it is very unlikely that decaying corpses would have been left amongst inhabited houses, it does seem possible that there was a final massacre at Mohenjo-Daro, after which the city was abandoned. The attraction of seeing this slaughter as the work of the Aryans is obvious, but there are difficulties in this interpretation. The invading *Aryas* must have come into India from the north-west (linguistically there is no other direction they could have come from) and in doing so they must have come first to the Punjab. Why then does the only evidence we have for a violent encounter come from Mohenjo-Daro in the Sind province? Why have we found no skeletons littering the streets of the northern cities? Of course it is possible to argue that the site of Harappa itself was largely ransacked in the last century and that the existence of skeletons in the streets may simply not have been recorded. This is true, but it is special pleading. It seems to me that the absence of any evidence for massacres in the northern province is a very serious gap in the argument for the destruction of the Indus civilization by invading Aryan speakers.

It is perhaps unlikely that the fall of a civilization occupying a million square kilometres could be explained by one process alone. In any case, whatever the explanation may be, it is clear that at the moment we do not have sufficient evidence. We need much more work—more survey, more excavation, more radiocarbon dates, more study of both the cultural and the environmental evidence—to throw light on all aspects of this mystery.

Valleys in the mountainous land mass between Mesopotamia and the Indus Valley sheltered urban centres of their own.

Chapter VII Between Tigris and Indus

This chapter is concerned with the regions which lie between the two main civilizations described in this book, those of Mesopotamia and the Indus Valley. Urban centres arose in the third millennium BC in several parts of this vast area, both in the river valleys which dissect the mountain and plateau regions of the land block between the two civilizations and on the coasts and islands of the sea that connected them in the south. Here I shall consider three main areas: Iran and Afghanistan, the Persian Gulf and southern Turkmenia (Soviet Central Asia).

Iran and Afghanistan

In Iran the growth of urban life took different forms in the lowland and highland zones. The low-lying region of Khuzistan in south-west Iran, particularly the area known as Susiana around the site of Susa, is geographically very similar to that of lower Mesopotamia. It is separated from the Tigris river system by only a low divide and both in prehistoric and historic times there were close relationships between this area and southern Mesopotamia. In historic times Susiana was part of the kingdom of Elam. In prehistoric times it had a regional cultural variant of its own and the development of urban life took a course parallel to and approximately contemporary with that of Sumer.

On the site of Susa itself, excavated by the French from 1897 to the present day, a series of phases has been recognized. In the earliest, which was contemporary with the Early Uruk period in Mesopotamia, the site was already a small town and technology had reached a high level of achievement: chert and obsidian were finely worked into knives and arrowheads, copper was used for axes, chisels, needles and mirrors; imported lapis lazuli and manufactured faience were used for beads. All these may have been produced by specialist craftsmen. It is sometimes suggested that even the pottery may have been made by full-time specialists; although the potter's wheel was not yet in use, the painted pottery was of very fine quality. Stamp seals were already current.

In the succeeding phase, correlated with the late Uruk period of prehistoric Sumer, painted pottery went out of fashion, but the potter's wheel came into use and the craft was now almost certainly organized on an industrial basis by professional potters. Some of the vessel forms are very similar to late Uruk pots from Sumer and it is possible that the potter's wheel was introduced from there. The next phase, which was approximately contemporary with the protoliterate phase in Sumer, saw the appearance of writing in Susiana. The earliest documents, which are account tablets, are written in the so-called Proto-Elamite script. Like the earliest writing in Sumer, this script is pictographic, but the symbols themselves are different from the earliest Sumerian writing; even when the same object is intended a different symbol is used. This indicates that the practice of writing developed separately in Susiana, though the *idea* of writing may have been borrowed from Sumer. The chronological evidence at present suggests that they developed more or less contemporaneously, though Mesopotamia may have had a slight priority. The Proto-Elamite script, which has not yet been deciphered, was used widely in Iran, not simply in Susiana, and it continued in use without perceptible change at least until the Sargonid period. Only under the Third Dynasty of Ur at the end of the third millennium BC was it replaced by Mesopotamian cuneiform, adapted to the local language, which is known as Anzanite.

The succeeding Susa phase seems to have been contemporary with the Early Dynastic period in Mesopotamia and, as in Mesopotamia, the first royal graves in Susiana appear now, suggesting that kingship developed at about the same time in both regions. Throughout this period many of the products of Susiana, especially those of metal, were very similar to those of Sumer, while others represent purely local traditions with no parallels in Mesopotamia, such as the monochrome painted pottery. This picture, which is built up from the archaeological evidence, of a largely independent kingdom in Susiana with, however, close cultural and commercial contacts with Sumer is also supported by the Mesopotamian documents. The kingdom of Elam and the Elamites are often mentioned in Sumerian and later Mesopotamian tablets, usually as enemies and sometimes as vassals of one or more of the Mesopotamian cities. But the Sumerians were not always the victors in their conflicts with the Elamites: Elamite kings held sway over Sumer for a brief period during Early Dynastic times and it was Elamite invaders who destroyed the ancient city of Ur around 2000 BC, bringing the Third Dynasty of Ur and with it the Sumerian renaissance to a final end. Much later in Mesopotamian history Elamite invaders brought the Kassite dynasty to an end in about 1170 BC, carrying back with them to Susa as trophies some of the most

Susa lay not far to the east of Mesopotamia in what was later to become the kingdom of Elam. Urban life developed there at about the same time and about the same pace as it did in Sumer. Technology reached a high level and pottery may have been made by specialist craftsmen even in the first phases of the town's history. The early, painted pottery (above and right) is hand-thrown.

prized possessions of Babylon, including the stone stele bearing the law code of Hammurabi and the statue of Marduk, the patron deity of Babylon.

The development of civilized life in Susiana can be regarded either as parallel to or as part of the Urban Revolution in southern Mesopotamia. Whatever the degree of direct influence from Sumer, it is clear that a similar process in a similar environment produced a closely comparable end-product. We do not need any new explanations for the rise of cities in Susiana. The situation is different, however, in the area to the east. Between the alluvial lowlands of Mesopotamia/Khuzistan and those of the Indus lie the mountain ranges and raised tablelands of Iran and Afghanistan. The few permanent rivers and the greater number of seasonal torrents that dissect the plateaux are not comparable with the great waterways of Mesopotamia and the Indus area. The quantity of water transported is much less and the resulting flood plains much smaller: it is not an environment that could support the kind of population for which we have evidence in the great civilizations of the third millennium BC. However, the area was not a hostile one for prehistoric settlement: the valleys and the desert oases were relatively fertile and, unlike the situation in the large alluvial plains, the raw materials desired by prehistoric man — timber, building stone, metal ores, precious and semi-precious stones etc. — were generally available. The archaeological evidence in fact suggests that the whole area was, in prehistoric terms, relatively densely settled. Settlement mounds, known as tells or tepes, occur in almost all the major valleys between Iraq and Pakistan in one direction and between the Caspian Sea and the Indian Ocean in the other and many that have been explored are known to have been occupied in the period with which we are concerned here, the fourth and third millennia BC. Most of these settlements were probably simply large and prosperous villages, but recent excavations have shown that some at least must be regarded as true towns. Among the most important are the sites of Tepe Yahya south of Kerman in southern Iran, Tepe Malyan north of Shiraz, Shahr-i Sokhta in Iranian Sistan on the border with Afghanistan, and Mundigak in southern Afghanistan itself. The sites were large centres of concentrated population: Shahr-i Sokhta, the largest of the sites, covers more than 100 hectares and is estimated to have housed some 20,000 people. Not all the sites have yielded evidence of literacy, but inscribed clay tablets have been found on a surprising number of sites: at Godin Tepe and Sialk in north-west Iran, and at Tepe Yahya, Tal-i Iblis and Tepe Malyan in the south. All the tablets appear to be account tablets and they are all in the pictographic Proto-Elamite script which, as we have seen, was used and perhaps invented in Susiana. This script appears at Tepe Yahya in the phase of that site dated by Carbon-14 to about 3500–3000 BC ($c.$ 2800–2300 bc) and is therefore approximately contemporary with the late Uruk and Jamdat Nasr (protoliterate) phases in Mesopotamia. This makes the Proto-Elamite script virtually as early as the earliest pictographic writing in Mesopotamia, although the tablets from Uruk are probably earlier than 3500 BC.

As well as evidence of urban conglomerations of population and of writing in the late fourth and third millennia BC, we have evidence of a considerable degree of economic specialization and of social stratification. Rich burials have been excavated at Shahr-i Sokhta and at Shah-dad, north-east of Kerman, belonging to phases contemporary with the Early Dynastic period of Mesopotamia. Those of Shah-dad have yielded bronze shaft-hole axes, necklaces of lapis lazuli, carnelian, turquoise and shell beads, silver and bronze cylinder seals and bowls of carved steatite and of alabaster. These indicate a high level both of craft specialization and of the accumulation of wealth by an elite class.

Unlike the situation in the civilizations of Egypt, Mesopotamia and the Indus, these cities of highland Iran and Afghanistan did not form part of a unified economic system. It seems that each valley supported a single large urban centre with a number of much smaller satellite communities and that, although there were trading connections between the different regions, each formed a distinct economic and cultural unit of its own. These small units, though clearly able for a time to support large, wealthy and highly organized societies, were much weaker than the vast civilizations of the alluvial lowlands. Isolated in their individual valleys, they were vulnerable both to environmental pressures, such as alterations in the river's course, and to cultural ones, such as changes in trading patterns. In fact urban life seems to have come to an end in most of the region at about the end of the third millennium BC. Sites such as Tepe Yahya, Shahr-i Sokhta and Mundigak were either abandoned altogether or reverted to a village level of existence and urban life did not reappear in highland Iran until the first millennium BC.

If the decline of urbanism in highland Iran is an interesting pheno-menon, so indeed is its original growth. It is clear that it did not arise on the same kind of basis as in the alluvial valleys of Mesopotamia and the Indus. We must look for some different explanation. The key seems to lie in the existence within the highland zone of the raw materials which were so much in demand in Mesopotamia and to a lesser extent in the Indus Valley also. We have evidence that Shahr-i Sokhta was acting as an inter-mediary in the trade in lapis lazuli between its source in the Badakshan area of northern Afghanistan and the Mesopotamian market. A lapis lazuli working area has been excavated on this site and has yielded thousands of tiny flint tools on which, when viewed under the microscope, can still be seen traces of the blue dust from the lapis lazuli. The site of Tepe Yahya was equally clearly involved in trade in steatite (soapstone), probably from a local quarry. Thousands of finished and unfinished objects and fragments have been found on the site, including beads, buttons, cylinder

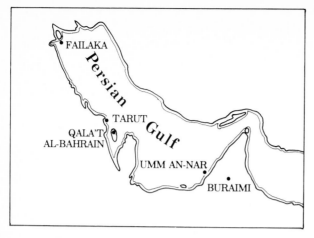

Links between Mesopo-
tamia and the Indus were
maintained by sea as
well as overland. Trading
stations opened up along
the Persian Gulf whose
north-west coast, with a
centre on Bahrain, was
probably the land of Dil-
mun, one of three regions
with which overseas trade
is recorded on the tablets.

seals, figurines and both plain and decorated bowls. Evidence from other sites is not so clear, but it is likely that sources of metal ores and turquoise were also being exploited. It seems probable that the growth of towns in the valleys of highland Iran was based on the exploitation of the demand for these raw materials in the civilizations of the alluvial lowlands. The whole question of trade and the rise of urbanism will be discussed further in chapter 9.

The Persian Gulf

When we discussed the trading activities of the Indus civilization we noted that various Sumerian documents (the earliest is in fact a tablet of Ur-nanshe, king of Lagash, in about 2520 BC) refer to trade between Sumer and three regions all reached by sea: Dilmun, Magan and Meluhha. And, as we have seen, most scholars now think that Meluhha refers to the area of the Indus civilization itself, Magan to the areas on both sides of the Strait of Hormuz (the Oman peninsula on one side and the Persian coast of the Makran on the other), while Dilmun is identified with the Arabian coast from the northern end of the Gulf to the island of Bahrain, with its centre on Bahrain. Sumerologists studying the tablets had speculated about the location of these lands for many decades, but until the early 1950s there was no archaeological evidence for third millennium BC settlements on the coasts or islands between southern Mesopotamia and the western flank of the Indus area. However, since 1953 a series of Danish expeditions to the Persian Gulf has begun to fill in this major blank in the archaeological record for western Asia. They have found a number of very important sites ranging geographically over the whole length of the Arabian side of the Gulf and in time from the Neolithic period to the sixteenth century AD. Here I shall mention only the third millennium BC sites relevant to the present discussion.

The Persian Gulf towns produced their own version of the Indus Valley stamp seals, distinctive discs of steatite (right), one of which has been found inscribed in the Indus script. Indus imports have been found on Bahrain where a stone-built town with a perimeter wall (below) has been identified as part of the Mesopotamians' land of Dilmun.

On the island of Bahrain itself the Danes have excavated a town site at Qala'at al-Bahrain at the northern end of the island. The first and second phases of this town of stone houses covered an area of about 17 hectares and are dated by the excavators to the later part of the third and the beginning of the second millennium BC and are identified as part of the land of Dilmun, recorded in the Sumerian tablets. A few kilometres west of Qala'at al-Bahrain is the site of Barbar, where the Danish expedition has excavated a complex temple building belonging to the same period as the early city at Qala'at al-Bahrain (labelled 'Early Dilmun' period). It is possible that this temple was not an isolated sanctuary, but itself part of a town—though the surrounding remains have not yet been investigated. Another settlement of the Early Dilmun period has been excavated on the tiny island of Failaka at the top end of the Persian Gulf, off Kuwait. Moreover, sherds of a distinctive kind of pottery characteristic of the Early Dilmun period have been found on the surface of a site on the island of Tarut and also on a site in the Hofuf oasis, some 90 kilometres inland, both in the territory of Saudi Arabia. These finds suggest that the land occupied by the Dilmun culture was quite extensive.

The material from these Early Dilmun sites forms a distinct regional culture with no *close* connections with that of any other area of western Asia. The most interesting of its products are the circular steatite stamp seals of the type labelled 'Persian Gulf seals'. As we have seen, these are closely related to those of the Indus civilization but were probably made somewhere in the Persian Gulf itself. The settlement on Failaka has produced many more of these seals than any other site and a single seal from here bears an inscription in the Indus script. Other evidence for contact with the Indus civilization comes in the form of a few actual imports from the Indus area found on Bahrain. Interestingly enough there are no identifiable *Mesopotamian* imports on Bahrain or Failaka, though the latter is less than one day's sail from the southern Mesopotamian cities. There is evidence for contact, however: a few objects have a rather Sumerian appearance: for example the little bronze figurine of a man in a suppliant posture from the Barbar temple. Moreover, the Mesopotamian cuneiform script and the Akkadian language were in use in both Failaka and Bahrain, though very few inscriptions have yet been found (a few from Failaka and one only from Bahrain). In addition a few Persian Gulf seals have been found, along with Indus ones, on the Mesopotamian site of Ur.

In addition to the sites of the Dilmun culture, the Danes have excavated two important sites further south in the Persian Gulf. The first is a settlement and a cemetery of chamber tombs on Umm an-Nar, a small island off the west coast of Abu Dhabi on the Oman peninsula. The second is a series of settlements and chamber tombs of the same culture in the Buraimi oasis in the middle of Oman. The so-called Umm an-Nar culture appears to be earlier than the Early Dilmun culture on

Bahrain, since sherds of Umm an-Nar pottery were found at the bottom of the sequence at Qala'at al-Bahrain below structures of the first city there. It is therefore dated by the excavators to the early part of the third millennium BC, though this date is regarded as too early by some other scholars. The excavators also suggest that the Umm an-Nar culture can be identified with the Magan of the Sumerian documents, but this is based on much flimsier grounds than the identification of the towns of Bahrain and adjacent areas with Dilmun.

If we put together the evidence of the Mesopotamian documents and the connections between Bahrain and Failaka and both Mesopotamia and the Indus civilization, a coherent picture begins to emerge. It seems likely that Bahrain, Failaka and perhaps towns in Saudi Arabia too were involved in maritime trade between the Indian Ocean areas and Mesopotamia. The absence of more than a handful of recognizable imports or exports in the archaeological record suggests that the bulk of the trade was in perishable goods. We made a similar deduction in the case of the Indus civilization's trade and it receives support from the Mesopotamian documents, which tell us that the Sumerian cities were importing raw materials such as metal ores, timber and precious and semi-precious stones and exporting food such as barley and vegetable oils and perishable manufactured goods such as woollen textiles. Dilmun itself appears in the documents mainly as an entrepôt, but is described also as exporting dates and pearls of its own. It seems likely that the growth of towns in the Persian Gulf paralleled that in the highlands of Iran, exploiting in the same way the Mesopotamian market for raw materials, available in this case through maritime trade via the Persian Gulf.

Turkmenia

The last area of western Asia in which archaeologists have found evidence for the growth of towns in the third millennium BC is southern Turkmenia. Unlike most of the areas which supported urban life at this time, Turkmenia is a land-locked country with no easy access to the outside world. Its two main rivers, the Amu Darya and the Syr Darya, do not flow out into any sea but peter out in the desert. As a result productive agriculture was limited to enclosed inland basins and early civilization in this area was centred on small oases rather than large river systems—much as we have seen in the other land-locked regions of highland Iran and Afghanistan.

Southern Turkmenia supported prosperous agricultural villages from the sixth to the fourth millennia BC, but in the third millennium there was a concentration of population into fewer, larger settlements. This was accompanied by the appearance of monumental architecture and evidence for both economic specialization in craft practice and social differentiation. Widespread trade is also attested and in addition there are hints of incipient

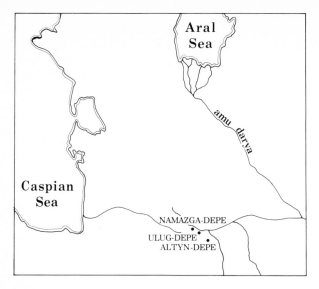

Settlements in Turkmenia developed into towns in the third millennium BC as the populations of formerly scattered oases began to group themselves into fewer, larger communities. But, with only small areas of productive land and rivers that continually shifted course, this land-locked country was unable to sustain indefinite urban expansion.

literacy. The development of these towns with their accompanying economic and social structure is rather inadequately dated. The beginnings of urban development belong to the local Early Bronze Age. This has a radiocarbon date from a late stage of about 2100 bc, which gives a corrected date of before about 2500 BC. The fully urban Middle Bronze Age has no radiocarbon dates but parallels in and possibly imports from the Indus civilization, for which we have dates of about 2400–1900 BC for the mature phase. At the moment it seems probable that the early period of urban development falls into the first half of the third millennium BC, the later period in the second half.

The two main settlements of the Bronze Age in Turkmenia are Namazga-depe and Altyn-depe. In the course of the third millennium BC these developed from small villages into substantial towns covering 70 and 50 hectares respectively. A third large town may have existed at Ulug-depe. These towns were surrounded by small villages of 1–2 hectares, scattered around the urban centres over areas with a radius of about 30 kilometres. The architectural features of the towns include remains of perimeter walls, compounds of large houses and monumental structures. The most impressive structure is at Altyn-depe, where a monumental tower-platform covering an area of 27·5 × 10·5 metres has been excavated. The outer façade of the tower was decorated with projecting pilasters and it is speculated that, as in Mesopotamia, it may have supported a temple.

The evidence for economic specialization is convincing. The potter's wheel was in use and on the so-called 'Craftsmen's Hill' at Altyn-depe a whole potters' quarter has been excavated, complete with houses, workshop and two-tiered potters' kilns. The kilns were producing not only pottery vessels but animal and human figurines also. Metallurgy was well

156

Evidence of incipient literacy in the first Turkmenian towns has been found in the form of scratched signs on clay figurines (on the woman's skirt *below*) and on a fragment of a single clay tablet (*right*).

developed and was presumably in the hands of specialist smiths: copper was alloyed with arsenic and with lead while both gold and silver were also worked. Other products probably made by specialists are stamp seals of bronze, silver, stone and baked clay, while jewellers made beads out of faience, agate, carnelian and lapis lazuli. That increasing economic specialization was accompanied by increasing social differentiation is suggested by the occurrence of wealthy graves. The so-called 'priestess' grave' at Altyn-depe contained a skeleton whose left hand was covered with gold rings and rested on two female figurines; elsewhere in the grave were the remains of one or more necklaces made of about 100 beads of agate, carnelian and lapis lazuli with gold binding and of paste with gold plating. Also in the grave was a seal in the shape of a fantastic three-headed beast of prey. By contrast the burials, presumably of artisans, found in graves under the floors of houses in the potters' quarter on 'Craftsmen's Hill' had no grave goods at all.

Archaeological evidence indicates that the Turkmenian towns, like those elsewhere in western Asia, were involved in wide-ranging trading activities. Many raw materials, such as metals (both native metals and ores) and semi-precious stones must have been imported, since sources do not exist within Turkmenia. We do not know, however, from which of the known sources of these raw materials the Turkmenian towns were drawing their supplies. As far as manufactured goods are concerned the only objects identified as actual imports by the excavators all come from a single hoard found at Altyn-depe. A grey-ware jug is thought to be an import from northern Iran while three ivory rods decorated with incised circles and some square and oval ivory gaming counters are regarded as imports from the Indus civilization. No imports from Mesopotamia have been recognized. What the Turkmenian towns were exporting we do not know; Turkmenian products have not been identified elsewhere in western Asia, so it seems that we can rule out manufactured goods or at least those made of imperishable materials. The area is not well supplied with raw materials, so it seems likely that they exported foodstuffs or other perishable products.

The evidence for incipient literacy comes in the form of a series of scratched signs on female figurines made of clay and in one case on a fragmentary clay tablet. The signs are repetitive and fall into six main groups. They clearly represent a well established system of symbols; because of their occurrence on the female figurines it is thought that they are associated with religious cult. These symbols cannot be regarded as a written language, but they may represent an early stage in the development of writing. Of course if a more advanced system had been developed for book-keeping purposes, a different writing material might have been employed and if this was of wood, skin or any other perishable material, we should have no surviving trace of it.

Trade accounted for the rise of many towns between Mesopotamia and the Indus, especially trade in lapis lazuli, a blue stone much favoured by the Sumerians. ▶

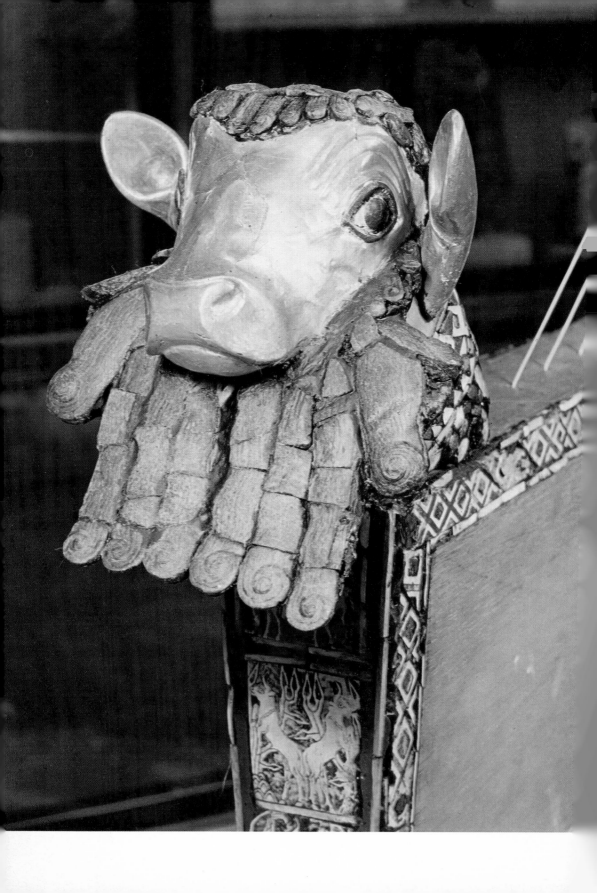

Turkmenian urbanism, like that of highland Iran, reached its peak in the second half of the third millennium BC and thereafter began to decline. In the Late Bronze Age (Namazga VI period) there was a marked decline in the size of the settlement at Namazga-depe and Altyn-depe was probably abandoned altogether. Most settlements of this period were only 1·5–2 hectares in size and economy reverted to a village level. The reasons for this decline may have been largely environmental. The rather small inland basins with their rivers liable to frequent shifts in course may have been unable to sustain continuous urban growth over very long periods. And it is one of the features of urbanism that when towns cease to expand they tend not to remain static but to shrink. Indeed it seems that in western Asia only the very large alluvial plains were able to support indefinite urban growth and even the vast Indus Valley could not maintain its civilization beyond the early part of the second millennium BC. The smaller urban developments of Turkmenia, highland Iran and Afghanistan and perhaps the Persian Gulf also, failed to maintain the momentum of further expansion and declined into village economies without ever reaching the peaks of development attained in Egypt, Mesopotamia and the Indus Valley.

The present explanation for the rise of towns in highland Iran and the Persian Gulf does not seem to apply to Turkmenia however. Turkmenia is not well supplied with raw materials and there is no evidence for the exploitation of any particular local commodity. Moreover, there is no evidence of trade of any kind with Mesopotamia and very little with the Indus Valley. It is possible to trace an uninterrupted development of culture and society from the earliest farming communities in the area and it seems most likely that we are dealing here with an independent centre of urban growth, admittedly smaller than, but not subsidiary to, the large civilizations of Mesopotamia and the Indus.

◀ *Lapis lazuli on a calf's head on a lyre from Ur is used with gold that would have been imported from Elam or from Syria.*

Chapter VIII   Precursors of the First Cities

In this chapter we are concerned with the background to the development of civilization in western Asia. As it happens, this area of the world has been the scene of much concentrated archaeological work in the last quarter of a century and the main focus on this work has been the elucidation of two major developments in the prehistory of man. The first of these is the transition from an economy based on hunting and gathering to one based on the cultivation of crops and the breeding of animals, which Childe called the Neolithic or Food-producing Revolution. The second is the development of urban civilization, Childe's Urban Revolution, which is the subject matter of this book. In fact the accomplishment of the first 'revolution' was a necessary precondition for the achievement of the second, since the high population densities of urban communities could be supported only by a secure and productive food supply. The wild food resources of even very favourable areas can rarely support population densities higher than one person per 10 square kilometres, whereas we estimated that Early Dynastic Sumer had a population concentration two hundred times greater than this (that is to say, 20 people per square kilometre). In this chapter we are going to consider the development of farming in western Asia, which set the stage for the later development of urban civilization.

The origins of farming

If we were to look at the map of western Asia at 12,000 bc, we should find a series of settlement sites along the shores of the Mediterranean and Caspian Seas and along the flanks of the Zagros mountains in eastern Iraq and western Iran. The sites were mostly caves and rock shelters, though a few encampments in the open are known. None of the settlements was large and none seems to have been permanently occupied. They were probably used seasonally by small bands of nomadic hunter-gatherers, probably numbering no more than twenty people each. The alluvial lowlands were totally empty of human settlement at this time. The hunters and gatherers of this period exploited what has been called a 'broad spectrum' of edible wild products: although ungulates (hoofed mammals) provided about 90 per cent of the meat diet of these communities, they also caught and ate small game, fish, turtles, water fowl, partridge, terrestial and marine snails, freshwater mussels and crabs. We may guess that a comparable range of wild vegetable products was collected too, but there is little evidence for this.

At this time, in about 12,000 bc, the world was still in the last ice age (the Pleistocene period), although in Europe the ice sheets had begun their final retreat. Most of the Near East was not directly affected by glaciation, but the end of the Pleistocene brought climatic and vegetational changes to this area too. As the climate became warmer, the oak woodland belt, which during the late Pleistocene had occupied only very restricted areas, expanded over much of the upland Near East. This oak woodland belt supports dense stands of edible nuts (especially pistachio), fruits and wild cereal grasses; it also shelters flocks and herds of sheep, goats, gazelle and onagers. It was therefore very desirable territory for groups exploiting a 'broad spectrum' of wild food resources. Within this woodland belt flourished the wild ancestors of the early cultivated crops— wheat and barley—and the first animals to be domesticated for food— sheep and goat. Between 10,000 and 6000 bc communities in different areas of the Near East learnt to cultivate these crops and breed these animals. The archaeological evidence available at present allows us to follow these developments in three separate areas: along the flanks of the Zagros mountains, in the Levant and in southern Anatolia.

In the Zagros region sites have been studied in the north, in Iraqi Kurdistan, and in the south-west, in the plains of Khuzistan; the area between—Luristan—is less well understood, but some early farming sites are beginning to be excavated there. Kurdistan has produced the earliest evidence for domesticated animals anywhere: by about 9000 bc a small community at the site of Zawi Chemi Shanidar, probably occupied only seasonally, was keeping sheep, but also hunting wild animals and harvesting some crops, probably wild. In Khuzistan the development of farming has been studied in great detail on the plain of Deh Luran over a period of some two millennia beginning in about 7500 bc. Here we shall consider developments up to about 6000 bc. In the earliest cultural phase that has been recognized, in about 7500–6750 bc, settlement was already permanent; domesticated goats played a key role in the subsistence economy and there were a few domesticated sheep too, but hunting and fishing still provided major sources of animal protein; barley and two kinds of wheat were cultivated but provided only about one third of the total weight of plant food, the rest being made up by the seeds of wild grasses and of wild leguminous plants (of the clover-alfalfa type). In the second phase, in about 6750–6000 bc, the same domesticated animals and plants were present and hunting and fishing were still very important; the main change was a decline in the collection of wild plant foods, suggesting that cereal cultivation was proving a more successful way of obtaining such sustenance. At about the same time as this second phase in Khuzistan (which is named after the important site of Ali Kosh), there was a permanent village at Jarmo in Kurdistan, with an economy based on the cultivation of barley, two kinds of wheat and a variety of leguminous crops, as well as the rearing of goats and perhaps also pigs. There is no evidence anywhere in this area before 6000 bc of large communities, of economic specialization in craft practice or of social differentiation.

The situation was different in the Levant and in southern Anatolia. In these areas, unlike the Zagros zone, the cultivation of plants was more important than the domestication of animals and was apparently accomplished earlier. In the Levant (Syria, Lebanon, Palestine and Jordan) there was a Mesolithic culture named the Natufian in the eighth millennium bc; the Natufian population lived mainly by hunting gazelle (almost to the exclusion of all other species), but they also harvested wild cereals. By the seventh millennium bc the Natufian culture had been succeeded by the so-called Pre-pottery Neolithic A culture, recognized on the sites of Jericho and Beidha and giving evidence of the cultivation of wheat and barley, but no definite evidence of domesticated animals except the dog (which is usually thought to have been domesticated as a hunting companion rather than for food). Hunting and collecting of wild foods were still important. In this phase the settlement at Jericho was already a site of at least 4 hectares surrounded by massive defences, suggesting a community of some size and a considerable degree of social organization. Later in the seventh millennium the Pre-Pottery Neolithic B culture was characterized by improvements in agricultural practice. A greater variety of cereals was grown and leguminous crops were cultivated also. Domesticated goats may have been kept at Jericho and Beidha; elsewhere the animal part of the diet was still supplied exclusively by hunting.

The Anatolian development was different from that of both the other areas discussed—the Zagros and the Levant—but it was closer to that of the Levant in its decided emphasis on agriculture rather than on stockbreeding. In fact there is no archaeological evidence for the earliest stages in the development of farming in this area. The story begins in about 7000 bc with the establishment of a small but permanent settlement at Hacílar. The community there cultivated wheat, barley and leguminous crops such as lentils. They also hunted wild animals and they collected wild plant foods, but they do not seem to have kept domesticated animals except for dogs. By the middle of the seventh millennium bc the site of

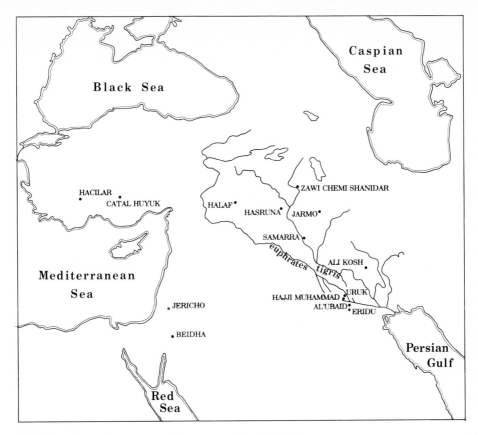

Early farming settlements, predecessors of the first cities.

Çatal Hüyük attests a well developed mixed farming economy, based on the cultivation of a variety of plants and the breeding of animals (sheep and goat and, later, cattle). The site of Çatal Hüyük was very large, much larger even than Jericho, covering about 13 hectares of land, and, to a degree far greater than any other early farming site, it has yielded evidence of secondary industries and of trade. I shall discuss the status of Jericho and Çatal Hüyük and their relevance to the later rise of city life in western Asia in the section after next.

Later developments in farming practice

By 6000 bc settled farming villages existed throughout the three zones we have discussed and doubtless elsewhere as well, for western Asia is still far from completely explored. There were sites on the upper Euphrates by this stage, but the alluvial lowlands were still unoccupied. By the following millennium cattle and swine had been added to the domesticated stock and there were other improvements in farming practice. As farming

165

became more efficient, hunting and the collection of wild plants declined in importance and these activities were further discouraged by the environmental changes produced by the early farming techniques (such as the destruction of tree cover). Successful farming was accompanied by a population expansion that is clearly documented in the archaeological record. By 5000 bc there were farming villages scattered over large areas of western Asia and indeed the farming economy had already begun to spread into Europe—but that is no part of the story of this book.

The early phases in the development of agriculture were characterized by cultivation which depends on natural rainfall for watering the crops. This type of farming, so-called dry-farming, which is the kind familiar to us in temperate Europe today, is perfectly efficient so long as the rainfall is adequate, but cannot be relied upon where the annual precipitation is less than about 250–300 millimetres. In western Asia this limited considerably the areas in which agriculture could be practised and it was for this reason that the alluvial lowlands were unoccupied during the early stages of the development of farming.

Some time before 5500 bc and perhaps even before 6000 bc some communities began to experiment with a technique that was to overcome this barrier: they began diverting stream courses to carry water to their fields. They were *irrigating*. As one might expect, this technique was developed not in the upland areas where rainfall was relatively heavy, but in the marginal zones where rainfall was insufficient to make dry-farming a really dependable method of food production. The earliest good evidence of irrigation comes from the lowlands of Khuzistan in south-west Iran, where the two phases of early farming already discussed were succeeded in about 5500 bc by a third which has produced evidence of irrigation agriculture. It is possible, however, that rudimentary irrigation may have been practised in the Levant even earlier. It has been suggested that it was in use at Beidha before 6000 bc and it is difficult to see how the community at Jericho could have managed without it, since the annual precipitation there is only 140 millimetres (it has been suggested that agriculture was *not* practised at Jericho and that the cultivated foodstuffs were imported from elsewhere, but this seems unlikely).

Irrigation was probably developed by the expanding early farming population as a method which made new land available for cultivation, but it had other effects too. It proved to be a much more productive method of farming. In Khuzistan it is claimed that the practice of irrigation agriculture today increases crop yields from 410 kilos per hectare to 615 kilos per hectare. Thus, at one and the same time, the new farming technology opened up new land for cultivation, including the fertile alluvium of southern Mesopotamia, and provided a means of obtaining greatly increased crop yields. This proved to be the economic basis on which the early civilizations could grow.

Jericho and Çatal Hüyük: early farming 'towns'

When Childe discussed the Urban Revolution he talked of 'the trans-formation of some tiny villages of self-sufficing farmers into populous cities, nourished by secondary industries and foreign trade and regularly organized as States'. Until the 1950s this seemed to be an accurate summary of the development he was describing, but excavations in the last quarter of a century have altered the picture dramatically. We have come to realize that the settlements of early farmers in western Asia were not necessarily 'tiny villages'; nor were they necessarily 'self-sufficing'. The two sites that most obviously fail to fall into this category are Jericho, which before 6500 bc was already a settlement of nearly 4 hectares surrounded by a massive defensive wall, and Çatal Hüyük, which only a little later occupied perhaps 13 hectares and was clearly involved in an organized trade in obsidian (a black volcanic glass which was much in demand for tools by prehistoric societies). Prehistorians frequently describe Jericho as a 'town' and Çatal Hüyük has even been described as a 'city'. Were there really towns in western Asia three millennia before the rise of cities in southern Mesopotamia?

The site of Jericho is situated in an oasis in the Jordanian desert north of the Dead Sea. The oasis is watered by an abundant natural spring—Elisha's Fountain—which makes it a very favourable area for settlement. The site was occupied, though not absolutely continuously, from the earliest settlement of the ninth or eighth millennium bc to the Bronze Age city which, the Bible tells us, fell to Joshua and the Israelites (probably some time after 1400 BC). At least by the seventh millennium bc settlement occupied an area of nearly 4 hectares and was surrounded by a town wall. These defences took the form of a rock-cut ditch, about 8 metres wide and 2·5 metres deep, on the inner edge of which was a high stone wall which had been faced originally with mud plaster. Behind this wall stood a massive circular stone tower, 8·5 metres in diameter and surviving to a height of about 7 metres. In the centre of the tower a roofed staircase made of great slabs of stone descended at an angle of about 30° from the vertical to a passage at the bottom. These impressive defences show evidence of at least three periods of building: only in the first phase were they free-standing on both faces; the later two were built up against deposits that had accumulated behind the first wall. This occupation was followed by an appreciable lapse of time during which the settlement went out of use; when it was reoccupied by people of a different culture the defences were not rebuilt but were covered first by debris and later by new dwellings. This settlement was not initially defended but at a later stage in its existence it too was given a massive defensive wall of stone. Its culture is much better known than that of its predecessors. At this stage the settlement still covered nearly 4 hectares and was occupied by densely packed buildings made up of several rectangular rooms (in contrast to the circular or elongated oval shape favoured earlier on), linked to others by courtyards and open spaces: no streets have been found. A Near Eastern town of this size today would house about 3000 people and a similar population has been suggested for Neolithic Jericho, though this estimate seems rather high to me.

Apart from the town walls, seventh-millennium bc Jericho did not boast any monumental architecture, but in its second phase several small buildings seem to have served as shrines. The most spectacular aspect of this culture was its skull cult: skulls removed from the rest of the skeleton had facial features restored in painted plaster and eyes inlaid with cowrie shells and were buried beneath house floors. These are usually, and probably rightly, interpreted as evidence of an ancestor cult, with the restored skulls being actual portraits of the deceased relatives.

Craft practice was well developed: pottery was not made, but fine carved limestone bowls were produced, while flint-workers made arrowheads, spearheads and components for multiple sickles, as well as knives and scrapers. Although all these products were of good quality they were within the range of production of early farming communities elsewhere and there is no reason to think that they were made by full-time specialists. The presence of obsidian at Jericho, shown by spectographic analysis to have come from an Anatolian source, indicates that the community here was participating in long-distance trade, but the quantities involved were so small that the trade cannot have been vital. As far as craft specialization and long-distance trade are concerned, Jericho was not exceptional among farming communities of the eighth and seventh millennia bc. What was remarkable about it was its size and its massive fortifications.

The site of Çatal Hüyük on the Konya plain in southern Anatolia was occupied from about 6500 to about 5500 bc. The whole site covers about 13 hectares, but we do not know to what extent it was occupied at any time within this period. In any case it probably had a population of several thousands. The buildings were made of clusters of adjoining rooms and were connected to each other by yards; as at Jericho there were no streets. The settlement had no specially constructed town wall, but, because the buildings had no doors (they were entered through the roof), the outside of the settlement presented a solid blank wall, which must have acted effectively as a defensive wall. Excavations at Çatal Hüyük have yielded clear evidence of both craft specialization and social stratification. The evidence for craft specialization comes in the quality and quantity of the products themselves: no workshops or working areas have yet been discovered, but they are assumed to lie somewhere under the 12 hectares of the mound which are still untouched by excavation. The crafts for which we have evidence of both quality and quantity of production are numerous. Workers in flint and obsidian produced pressure-flaked arrowheads, daggers, spearheads, knives, sickles, scrapers and borers, as well as

The oasis of Jericho in the Jordanian desert, with the mound of the first town in the foreground, the modern city in the middle distance and the Dead Sea beyond. At Jericho a powerful spring and exceptional fertility supported a limited urban development in the seventh millennium bc. At Çatal Hüyük in Turkey, another settlement that showed signs of urbanism in the period preceding the rise of true cities in western Asia, wealth was based on trade in obsidian.

beautiful round mirrors of polished obsidian. Jewellers made beads for necklaces, armlets, bracelets and anklets out of stone, shell, chalk, clay, mother-of-pearl and even copper and lead; they also made carved pendants and used stone inlays. Workers in ground stone made axes, adzes, polishers, grinders, chisels, maceheads and palettes, the latter used for the preparation of cosmetics. Workers in bone made awls, punches, knives, scrapers, ladles, spoons, bowls, scoops, spatulas, bodkins, belt-hooks, toggles, pins and cosmetic sticks. Wood-carvers made beautiful bowls and boxes; textile-workers wove woollen cloth and, if we are to judge by the wall paintings, they were already making woven rugs or kilims in bright colours, just as they do today. Basket-makers made containers and mats. In the later stages there were potters too: an attempt to introduce pottery at an earlier stage seems to have failed because the pottery was not good enough to compete with wooden containers or baskets; good quality pottery came into use only after about 6000 bc. It seems likely that all these manufactures were produced by specialists and that some at least of these were full-time specialists. Also specialists were the artists who decorated the remarkable shrines for which this site has become famous: painted scenes of life and death, full of symbolism, some obvious, some obscure to us, adorned the walls while modelled animal heads (especially bulls' heads or bulls' horns on their own) and women's breasts, sometimes gruesomely harbouring within them vultures' skulls or other animal remains, were attached to walls or benches.

Evidence for social stratification comes both from the houses and the burials, which demonstrate marked differences in quality and in the lavishness with which they were equipped. Clearly there were rich and poor in this community, though there were probably no rigid divisions.

The source of Çatal Hüyük's exceptional wealth was its exploitation of the demand that existed throughout the Near East for the black volcanic glass, obsidian. Spectographic analysis has shown that obsidian from two sources in Anatolia (Açigol and Çiftlik) was in use on many Anatolian sites and was traded to the Levant, reaching even Jericho and Beidha in small quantities. Çatal Hüyük is situated not far from these sources and it seems probable that its population acted as middlemen in the trade in obsidian and grew rich on the profits.

There may have been other early farming settlements in western Asia that were very large or had communities practising some degree of economic specialization, but no sites have been excavated to date that compare with Jericho or Çatal Hüyük in these respects. What does it all amount to? And what relevance does it have to the later development of urbanism in Mesopotamia and areas further east? It is worth noting firstly that the developments on these two sites were isolated and secondly that they were different from one another; in the third place both sites lacked some of the features that characterized the later development of towns in Mesopotamia. Both Jericho and Çatal Hüyük were exceptionally large in the context of early farming settlements, but there the resemblance ends. The remarkable feature of Jericho is its massive defensive wall and ditch, which suggests a social organization with power in the hands of a central authority. At Çatal Hüyük we have no defensive wall or indeed any obvious public work; the 'urban' aspect of this site, apart from its size, is in the evidence for economic specialization and social differentiation. Both sites lacked some of the features which characterized the towns that developed in southern Mesopotamia three millennia later: streets, monumental public buildings and of course writing are all absent from the two sites we have been discussing. If we wish to call Jericho and Çatal Hüyük 'towns'— and I think we may do so in recognition of their unique features in the early farming context—we must recognize also that they were towns only in a limited sense of the word.

The precocious development documented on these two sites can perhaps be explained in terms of exploitation of exceptional local resources. I suggest that the growth of Jericho was based purely on agricultural wealth: the water of Elisha's Fountain, exploited by irrigation (which we deduced was necessary to practise agriculture here at all), raised productive crops on the fertile soils of the oasis, sufficient to support a population of several thousand. The growth of a central political authority, suggested by the existence of town defences, might have resulted simply from the population expansion: only very small communities can exist without some such form of organization. However, it is likely that there was some outside threat, against which the defences were erected, and such an external threat undoubtedly would have hastened the emergence of a central authority. Çatal Hüyük did not owe its wealth purely to agricultural success, but to the exploitation of Anatolian obsidian. However it is no accident that this community flourished not in the highlands close to the sources of obsidian, but in the fertile Konya plain to the south, where higher crop yields could be obtained. Çatal Hüyük did not depend on irrigation agriculture, but on productive dry-farming, but the end result was the same. Only intensive food production could support a large population and no quantity of obsidian or any other product could help a community expand and grow rich if there was insufficient food to feed the new specialist workers.

I am not saying that intensive food production was the *cause* of these precocious urban developments, but without it they certainly could not have occurred. In this respect the developments at Jericho and Çatal Hüyük provide a valid parallel to the later development of cities in Meso-potamia. However, unlike the later development, this early precocity did not reach the level of full civilization and indeed, after reaching a certain high point of development, the early towns began to decline. After about 5000 bc neither the Levant nor southern Anatolia supported more advanced communities than other parts of western Asia. There are many possible reasons why true city life did not develop at this stage. One of the most likely is the nature of the resources exploited by these communities. Jericho was isolated in its oasis. Çatal Hüyük was not restricted geographically, but it was dependent on the obsidian trade, which could probably only support one large community at this time. In both cases the resources allowed the growth of a single exceptionally large and organized community. But probably no single settlement could carry the momentum of economic growth through to the emergence of full civilization: this would have required the development of a much larger economic system based on the exploitation of a correspondingly larger natural environment. It is probably no accident that the three major civilizations of western Asia evolved in the very large alluvial systems of the Nile, the Tigris-Euphrates and the Indus. Smaller environmental regions of western Asia did support urban developments at a later date, but even then none reached the level of organization and achievement found in the three great civilizations.

There we shall leave speculation for the moment. For whatever reason, the precocious towns of Jericho and Çatal Hüyük failed to develop into true cities and when urban civilization *did* arise in western Asia, it did so on an entirely different basis. We shall now return to the story of the settlement of western Asia by early farming communities and to the events of the two millennia that preceded the emergence of civilization in southern Mesopotamia.

The prelude to the Urban Revolution

Before 6000 bc settlement in western Asia was limited to the areas where farming could be practised without irrigation, although, as we have seen, some communities were probably experimenting with irrigation before this date. However, when irrigation farming came into general use in the course of the sixth millennium bc, the alluvial lowlands were opened up for settlement for the first time. Northern Mesopotamia was rapidly and rather densely settled in the 500 years following 6000 bc, but farmers were slow to penetrate the marshy lands of the extreme south where civilization was eventually to emerge. No settlement has yet been found in southern Mesopotamia which can be dated before 5000 bc. During the same millennium, 6000–5000 bc, flourishing farming villages became established over large parts of the upland regions of western Asia. However, the largest and most successful communities were in the alluvial plains and it is in these areas that the major developments of the next two millennia occurred. It is probable that northern Mesopotamia was settled from the north-west, from Anatolia or northern Syria, since the early Mesopotamian cultures show strong connections with the Chalcolithic cultures of Anatolia, which succeeded the seventh millennium Neolithic culture we have seen at Çatal

Monumental buildings and even streets did not exist in seventh-millennium Jericho. Its main urban feature was a massive defensive wall of stone, one tower of which has been excavated.

A religious cult in Jericho included reverence for the skulls of the dead. Their facial features restored in plaster (left) and their eyes inlaid with cowrie shells (above), the skulls were buried beneath house floors.

Hüyük. By contrast, southern Mesopotamia was probably settled by people coming from the east, from Iran.

The earliest settlements in northern Mesopotamia belong to a culture labelled Hassuna-Samarra (after two different sites). They were flourishing farming villages, but no very advanced technological, economic or social developments have been noted here. Their most striking product was their painted pottery, especially the fine Samarra ware with its geometric patterns or bird, fish or animal designs executed in dark paint on a light background. The Hassuna communities imported obsidian as well as turquoise and perhaps amethyst which they used for beads.

The succeeding Halaf culture, which can be dated to about 5200–4500 bc, was characterized by more developed communities. The houses were larger and better built and one site, Arpachiyah, already had cobbled streets. Arpachiyah also produced remains of ten impressive vaulted beehive-shaped structures approached by long rectangular antechambers. They were made of *pisé* (compacted mud) on stone foundations. Their function is unknown but whether they were for religious or secular use, it is likely that they were public buildings—the earliest for which we have evidence in Mesopotamia. Technology was also more advanced than in the Hassuna-Samarra period. The Halafians were very probably metal-using; they made exceptionally fine polychrome painted pottery which was undoubtedly fired in proper kilns though it was still hand-made; they produced fine carved vessels, beads and amulets out of hard stone; certain steatite pendants were used to make impressions on lumps of clay—so becoming the first seals to be used in Mesopotamia. Trade brought obsidian and other commodities in quantity to the Halafian communities.

The Hassuna-Samarra and the Halaf cultures occurred in northern Mesopotamia only but the culture that succeeded the Halafian is found throughout the land in the middle of the fifth millennium bc. Indeed there is every reason to believe that this culture, which is named after the site of al'Ubaid near Ur, was southern Mesopotamian in origin. Certainly it appeared in the north as an intrusion that brought the Halafian culture to an apparently abrupt end. The earliest two phases of settlement in the south have been named after the sites of Eridu and Hajji Muhammad respectively, but they were of limited distribution and probably represent early phases in the development of the Ubaid culture proper. The Ubaid culture itself is found on many sites in southern Mesopotamia, but it occurs also throughout the north and in recent years typical Ubaid pottery has been found in areas to the south of Mesopotamia on both sides of the Persian Gulf, in Arabia and in Iran. The Ubaid culture represents an advance on the Halaf culture in several different spheres. The most striking innovation is the appearance of monumental religious buildings, the precursors of the great temples of the later Mesopotamian cities. Even the earliest settlement at Eridu had a small shrine and over this was constructed a series of 17 progressively larger and more impressive temples culminating in a ziggurat dating from the end of the third millennium bc. Temples occur on Ubaid sites in both southern and northern Mesopotamia and indeed temples have been found on *every* Ubaid site where a reasonably large area has been excavated. It is clear that the Ubaid settlements, which perhaps we may now call towns, were centred round a religious building like all their successors. It is probable that the economic role played by the temple in Early Dynastic Sumer was already in existence, at least in embryo. The Ubaid communities were certainly metal-using; they harnessed the wind to propel boats; and they made the first true stamp seals in Mesopotamia (in contrast to the seal pendants of the Halaf culture). They imported flint, obsidian and other stones and presumably metal in some form or other, but there is little evidence for trade in luxury articles. Nor is there much evidence for craft specialization.

The succeeding Uruk phase was already truly urban. Communities were much larger and the temples had become massive and spectacular monuments, representing very many man-hours of work. There were developments in craft practice too and some of the craftsmen were almost certainly specialists: the potters, for example, who produced the unpainted but wheel-made vessels of this period and probably also the metal smiths who now alloyed copper with lead and cast tools by the *cire perdue* technique. There may well have been other specialist craftsmen too, such as carpenters and leatherworkers. Wheeled vehicles were now in use and animals (oxen and perhaps onagers) were harnessed to pull them. Trade brought supplies of copper, gold, silver and lead and various stones, including the precious lapis lazuli that had to come all the way from northern Afghanistan. An important invention of the Uruk period, made late in Uruk times, was the cylinder seal, which was to remain current in Mesopotamia from the Uruk period to late Babylonian times. The most important invention of this period, however, was that of writing, which allows us to classify late Uruk society as truly 'civilized'.

The urban development of the Uruk period is clearly rooted in the achievements of the preceding Ubaid period. If we are to understand the events that led up to the emergence of civilization in southern Mesopotamia, it is upon this culture that we must first focus our attention. It represents the first specific adaptation to the south Mesopotamian environment and it bore within it the seeds of the later growth. With this in mind, in the last chapter I shall attempt to discuss the reasons for the growth of civilization in this area.

Chapter IX The Origins of Civilization

For more than half a century, since knowledge of Sumerian civilization first became widespread, scholars have been trying to explain why the world's first cities arose in the alluvial plain of southern Mesopotamia in the fourth millennium bc. The explanations offered by scholars at an earlier stage were often simplistic, citing single factors such as the practice of irrigation as the sole or main cause of the rise of cities. Modern scholars, who are still much preoccupied with this problem, describe the rise of civilization as the result of the interaction of a number of different factors. Here I shall not attempt to list all the explanations that have been suggested (and there are almost as many as there are scholars working on the problem), nor shall I settle for one single explanation which seems particularly plausible to me. Instead I shall outline the main factors that were probably relevant to the emergence of civilization and suggest how they may have interacted. They are environment and subsistence economy; population; technology; trade; and economic and social organization. I shall deal in the first instance with the earliest manifestation of civilization in southern Mesopotamia and discuss the other areas separately later.

Environment and subsistence economy
The natural environment played an important role in the emergence of civilization. It can be no accident that the three great early civilizations of Egypt, Mesopotamia and the Indus arose in large alluvial plains and that no other kind of environment supported comparable civilization for several millennia afterwards. Interestingly enough, the fourth major ancient civilization of the Old World, the Shang civilization of China, arose in the second millennium bc on a comparable alluvial plain, that of the Huang-Ho or Yellow River. As we have already seen, the virtue of the alluvial plains was that, when irrigated, they could produce very high

crop yields. I have emphasized before that without intensive food production it was impossible to support the high population densities associated with urban life; and without irrigation it was impossible in the ancient world, lacking the benefits of later technological developments, to achieve intensive food production. In this sense the earlier generation of scholars, such as Childe and Frankfort, were quite right to emphasize the crucial role of irrigation in the development of civilization. But it is one thing to say that without irrigation civilization would not have emerged in western Asia at this time—which few scholars would dispute—and quite another to say that irrigation was the main *cause* of the development of civilization.

Let us look a little closer at the effects of the introduction of irrigation. We have already noted two major results: it allowed the settlement of the alluvial lowlands for the first time and it allowed the production of very high crop yields. Both these factors were obviously of great importance for the emergence of civilization, but there was a third factor which may have been of equal if less obvious importance. This arises from the fact that, although irrigation produces much higher yields than dry-farming (an increase of more than 50 per cent if we can use modern Iranian analogies), a much smaller percentage of the land is suitable for irrigation agriculture than for dry-farming. In modern Iran, for instance, 10 per cent of the land is used for arable, but only 1 per cent is irrigated and on this 1 per cent grows about 30 per cent of the annual crop of the country. Thus, although irrigation farming was undoubtedly a more efficient technique than had been used previously, it was applicable to a much more restricted area. This immediately gave rise to big differences in the quality and value of agricultural land, the small percentage of irrigable land being obviously much more valuable than the larger area that could not be irrigated. Since populations on the alluvial plains were large, it is unlikely that there would have been sufficient high quality irrigable land for all; instead the best land would be in the hands of a small minority (whether owning it privately or on behalf of an institution such as the temple). This is in contrast to the conditions in the uplands where farming was first developed; here smaller populations exploiting a larger amount of land of approximately equal farming quality would have lived in a situation of 'equality of opportunity' (an equality provided by nature, not created by man). It seems likely that these differences in the value of farming land in the plains and the exploitation of the good land by a minority of the population provided the basis, or one of the bases, on which social stratification grew.

Irrigation was not the only aspect of the subsistence economy that contributed to the development of civilization. Another seems to have been the variety of subsistence activities practised. We know that, as well as growing cereal crops, the communities of southern Mesopotamia grew dates and other fruits, kept herds of domesticated animals, hunted the game of the plains and the marshy delta region and also caught fish in the rivers and lagoons. Now, such a diversity of activities is not easily practised by a single individual and it is likely that there was at an early date some degree of specialization of labour in subsistence activities. Simple farming communities usually practise some specialization according to sex and age, but in the larger societies of southern Mesopotamia it seems that there was a more organized division of labour, probably co-ordinated by the central authority whose existence we have deduced from the appearance of monumental temples in the Ubaid period and smaller shrines even in the earlier Proto-Ubaid (Eridu and Hajji Muhammad) phase.

To summarize, we might say that the alluvial plain provided the environment on which, if properly exploited, cities could grow. The sub-sistence economy, based on irrigation agriculture supplemented by the exploitation of a variety of other food sources, provided the intensive food production necessary for the support of urban populations. Moreover the differences in value in agricultural land that arose from the practice of irrigation provided the basis for the development of social stratification. Finally, the variety of subsistence activities practised provided the basis for the development of a complex division of labour.

Population

There is a current vogue for invoking population expansion and population pressure as causes of many important developments in prehistory. Predict-ably there is a school of thought that maintains that it was the pressure of an expanding population within a restricted area that gave rise to civilization in southern Mesopotamia. Another school maintains, however, that large population increases followed rather than preceded the Urban Revolution. What is the evidence?

A dramatic increase in population was one of the results of the earlier 'Food-producing Revolution', the development of farming. Whereas the preceding hunting and gathering groups may have maintained an approxi-mate equilibrium between population and resources, the early farming societies were constantly growing, often beyond the carrying capacity of their environment. The reasons for this are disputed and need not bother us here: the dramatic population expansion that followed the development of farming is a fact which is clearly documented in the archaeological record. The permanent villages of the eighth, seventh and sixth millennia bc are larger in size than the seasonally occupied camps and shelters of the preceding millennia, there are many more of them and they occur in areas where there were no settlements at all in earlier periods; the size of cemeteries too, where they have been found, indicates larger populations. A further increase in population seems to have followed the introduction of irrigation. Calculations made by archaeologists working in the plains of Khuzistan suggest a population density of about 0·1 persons per square kilometre for late hunting and gathering communities, 1–2 people per square kilometre for early farmers and about 6 people per square kilometre after the introduction of irrigation.

Thus, it is certainly the case that population was increasing at a considerable rate in western Asia *before* the Urban Revolution; this is therefore a factor that must be considered as a possible cause of the Revolution. If it was a cause, however, it was not a simple case of more people leading to the growth of larger communities, which could then be classified as cities. Population expansion does not automatically lead to the growth of larger communities: in fact in prehistory the most common result of a community growing beyond a certain size was the hiving off of 'daughter communities' to establish new settlements elsewhere. This mechanism explains the geographical expansion of early farming villages and accounts for the rapidity with which the techniques of farming were spread not only over western Asia, but throughout temperate Europe also. However, there are circumstances in which an expanding population can lead to the growth of larger communities. One such circumstance is when the area available for settlement is restricted either by environmental factors or by the existence of already established communities in neighbouring areas *and* when this restricted area is able to produce sufficient food for a larger population. Now, this is exactly the combination of circumstances obtaining in southern Mesopotamia: the alluvial plain was restricted in area but was sufficiently fertile to be able to feed a large population. Thus the expanding population could be contained within the limited area and the result was larger communities and a higher population density over the whole area.

In fact the archaeological evidence for southern Mesopotamia suggests that this is what *did* happen in this area. Moreover it allows us to pinpoint the stage at which increasing population ceased to result in expansion outwards and started to be absorbed locally, resulting in larger communities. As we saw in the last chapter, the Ubaid culture occurred all over both southern and northern Mesopotamia and in parts of Arabia and southern Iran as well and the communities of this period were still of modest size. This suggests that the Ubaid culture was still one that solved the problem of population increase by the hiving off of daughter communities to settle elsewhere. By contrast the succeeding Uruk culture is found only in southern Mesopotamia and the communities of this period were already substantial towns. Clearly the Uruk communities were containing their population increase within a restricted zone, with the result that their settlements increased in size. By the protoliterate or Jamdat Nasr stage in the late fourth millennium BC this trend had become more marked and most of the major centres of the later Early Dynastic period were already large towns or cities. What was the difference between the Ubaid and the later cultures that allowed this difference in the way they dealt with their increasing population? Those scholars who favour purely demographic explanations maintain that the population pressure increased at this time to a point which forced the Uruk population to develop new methods of dealing with it. As well as the steady increase that had been continuing from the beginnings of settlement on the plain, there was an additional increase late in Uruk times. This was not the result of an increase in birth rate or any other strictly demographic factor, but of an environmental circumstance that had a similar effect. Survey in the area of Kish suggests that an eastern branch of the Euphrates river dried up at this time, forcing all the communities settled on this branch to move westwards to another channel of the river. The effect on those communities already established on this more westerly channel amounted to a large and very sudden population increase. However, it is not known whether this was a local phenomenon in the area of Kish or whether areas to the south were affected also.

Alternative explanations for the growth in community size in Uruk and Jamdat Nasr times are possible. The most likely involve the combination of natural population increase with other factors such as increasing efficiency in the subsistence economy. Just such an increase in efficiency is documented in the archaeological record in Jamdat Nasr times. A study of the settlement pattern in the Ur-Uruk-Eridu area of the extreme south shows a distinct change between the Uruk and the Jamdat Nasr phases. Uruk settlements are scattered along existing and former river courses, suggesting that irrigation was still of a primitive kind, based on diverting water from natural streams over small distances only. In the Jamdat Nasr period settlements appear in linear arrangements over areas where no natural water courses ever existed, suggesting that artificial canals were now in use. Such an increase in efficiency could well explain the difference in size between Uruk and Jamdat Nasr settlements and there may have been some comparable improvement in efficiency between the Ubaid and the Uruk periods, though obviously not one that has left such clear evidence in the settlement pattern.

What about the claim that the main population increase followed rather than preceded the Urban Revolution? This in fact appears to be the case: the difference in size between the huge Early Dynastic cities and the towns of the Uruk period is far greater than the difference between these towns and the earlier Ubaid villages or small towns. However, the actual size of the increase is not significant in this connection; what does matter is whether the increase was sufficient to precipitate any important economic or social change. I should summarize the situation as follows. It seems likely that population increase—in the context of a geographically restricted but very productive environment, exploited by irrigation agriculture—*did* play an important role in the development of civilization.

The relationship between an expanding population and economic specialization and social stratification will be discussed in the subsequent sections.

Technology

Just as a change in fashion has brought explanations based on population into vogue, so a corresponding change has made explanations based on technology unfashionable today. However, Childe considered the role played by improvements in technology important and certainly they cannot be ruled out of court without consideration. Childe was quite explicit about the role of technology. He wrote: 'Between 6000 and 3000 BC man has learnt to harness the force of oxen and of winds, he invents the plough, the wheeled cart, and the sailing boat, he discovers the chemical processes involved in smelting copper ores and the physical properties of metals, and he begins to work out an accurate solar calendar. He has thereby equipped himself for urban life, and prepares the way for a civilization . . .'. The major technological inventions regarded as important by Childe had indeed been made before the Urban Revolution, in some cases a long time before. These were the discovery of metallurgy, the invention of the wheel and the harnessing of animal and wind power. When discussing the role of these advances in technology in the development of civilization we must ask ourselves two questions. The first is: 'What effect would these inventions have had on the societies that developed them?'; and the second is: 'Could civilization have developed without them?'

There is no single or simple answer to the first question; clearly the new technological developments had several different direct results and many more potential ones. I shall concentrate on three areas they affected. Firstly they led directly to increased efficiency in primary production. Secondly they encouraged the growth of economic specialization. Thirdly they provided the means for the further development and elaboration of cultural life. All three factors are interrelated. The first result is more or less self-evident: technological improvements might be expected to lead to greater efficiency in the practice of the subsistence economy. For instance, metal tools are more efficient than stone ones: metal axes cut down trees faster than stone ones and metal sickles can harvest a crop faster than flint or clay ones. This comment, however, needs qualifying. Metal tools were not *that* much more efficient than stone ones; what made them so much more valuable was their durability. A stone axe becomes blunt rapidly and needs regrinding to sharpen it, a laborious process that reduces it considerably in size; moreover a stone axe may snap and when it does it has to be thrown away. A bronze axe takes longer to lose its edge and when it does it can be sharpened more easily than a stone axe;

182

it is unlikely to snap, but if it does, or when it gets very worn, it can be melted down and recast into a brand new tool. This advantage, appreciated by all prehistoric societies, was of overwhelming importance in the alluvial plains of southern Mesopotamia where all raw materials were at a premium. The harnessing of animal power had a direct effect on the efficiency of agriculture through the invention of the ox-drawn plough. Certainly invented before 3500 bc, perhaps much earlier, the plough pulled by oxen broke up the ground much more effectively and much faster then the manually operated digging stick or hoe. The effects of the introduction of wheeled vehicles and sailing boats on primary production were less direct, but by simplifying and accelerating the transport of goods, including food products, they facilitated the concentration of these products and their redistribution from a central store.

The way in which technological improvements encouraged economic specialization is also fairly obvious. The processes involved in the new techniques were much more complex than any used previously and it is likely that those who practised them were full-time specialists. Whereas many kinds of stone tool could be manufactured by almost anyone whenever a new one was needed, the production of metal tools required a knowledge of the complex processes of smelting and casting. The metal smiths who mastered these processes were almost certainly full-time specialists and not involved at all in the business of food production. A similar result followed the introduction of the principle of the wheel into the production of pottery. The potter's wheel, which came into use in Uruk times in southern Mesopotamia, increased the efficiency of pottery production, but made the process a more complicated one, which in all probability was in the hands of specialist potters. In a general sense increasing complexity in technology is bound to encourage economic specialization (although it is often difficult to estimate its degree from the archaeological evidence). A considerable degree of specialization means that a considerable number of people have to be supported out of the surplus food produced by those engaged in primary production. Thus only a community able to produce a considerable surplus of food can support a high level of technological development.

The third aspect of technological development I wish to discuss is the way in which it encourages the creation of new types of artefact and new activities, including many of a non-functional nature. Metal, for instance, could be used not only for better axes, adzes, sickles, knives, gouges, chisels and so on than could be made of stone, but also for totally new types of tools. It was only after the discovery of metallurgy, for instance, that saws or shears could be made and both these tools had great potential. Saws revolutionized carpentry and indeed may have been a necessary precondition for the invention of the wheel, while shears vastly increased efficiency in wool production (previously wool had to be plucked either

In peace-time, on one side of the Royal Standard from Ur, a king is enthroned among his nobles. On the other side, in war-time (above), he leads his troops against the enemy. Both sides illustrate the emergence in Early Dynastic Mesopotamia of social classes, one of the main features of urban life. One factor contributing to such social differentiation had been the very need for a military leader. This had been preceded by, and was later to encourage and increase, specialization in craft practice, another class-provoking phenomenon, of which an Akkadian seal (impression right) is a fine expression.

184

from the living animal or the dead fleece; with the invention of shears wool could be taken from the same animal over and over again without hurting the creature at all). Moreover, as well as for tools, metal could be used for goblets and plates, for necklaces, bracelets and diadems, for ornamental fittings for furniture or trappings for animal harness—many of which could not be made nearly so well, if at all, in the materials available previously. Similarly, wheeled vehicles can be everyday carts pulled by oxen or processional chariots pulled by thoroughbred horses. Sailing boats can carry cargoes of grain or royal parties on ceremonial voyages. These examples could be multiplied many times over; for instance, all these inventions have enormous military potential, which I have not considered here. Thus the technological inventions we have been considering opened up new avenues in many spheres of life including the practical, the military, the ceremonial and the recreational. Such developments would have contributed to increasing economic specialization.

We have looked at some of the effects that advances in technology had or may have had on the societies that developed them. We must now turn to our second question which was: 'Could civilization have developed without them?' In one sense we must answer 'yes' to this question: we know that some civilizations *did* develop without them. The Maya civilization of central America had no wheeled vehicles, no ploughs, no sailing boats, no domestic animals and no metal. Even the later Incas of Peru, who had the most highly developed of all the American civilizations in many ways, had no wheeled vehicles and though they used domesticated llamas as pack animals, they did not harness them to pull anything (not ploughs, carts or sledges); nor did they harness the wind to propel sailing boats. Yet these societies meet the criteria by which we defined civilization in chapter 1; clearly, the state of civilization could be attained in some cases without the aid of these technological developments. However, whether civilization could have developed in western Asia without their aid is another matter. We know that in this part of the world the technological developments *did* precede the Urban Revolution and to me it seems likely that without them the productive potential of the alluvial plains could not have been fully exploited.

Trade

Trade was another factor emphasized by Childe in his account of the emergence of city life in Mesopotamia. We have already seen how the alluvial plains lacked all mineral materials and even good building timber, so that many essential materials, as well as luxuries, had to be imported into Sumer, often from considerable distances. This meant the abandonment of the theoretical self-sufficiency of the early farming villages: the settlements of southern Mesopotamia could not survive without their

186

imported materials. The merchants involved in this trade must have been full-time specialists, for it would have been very difficult effectively to combine farming and long-distance commercial activities. And, because the trade was so vital to the existence of the Sumerian towns, the merchants would have been provided for, and doubtless well provided for, out of the community's surplus. We have already seen how the nature of the subsistence economy and the development of technology contributed to increasing economic specialization; the need for long-distance trade in raw materials not available locally also contributed to this process. The trade of this period could not be organized on the same basis as the obsidian trade among the farming villages of earlier times. Whereas those villages could manage without obsidian if supplies failed, the Sumerian towns needed an absolutely dependable supply of essential raw materials and trade had to be organized to produce such a reliable supply. The evidence for the Early Dynastic period is that all trading activities were controlled directly by the temple and the palace; the merchants were not private venturers, but were employees of the great organizations; imports went directly into their magazines and exports emanated from the same source. We may guess that in the earlier Predynastic period merchants were already 'State' employees, attached at this period only to the temple, since royal power had not yet developed. The need for an efficiently run trade thus contributed not only to increasing economic specialization, but also to the centralization of economic affairs. This will be discussed further below.

Social organization

The social and economic factors most frequently referred to in recent explanations for the rise of cities are the interrelated ones of economic specialization, social differentiation and the centralization of economic and political power. Earlier scholars tended to regard these developments as the *results* of the Urban Revolution, while those working on the problem today believe that they contributed to the accomplishment of the Revolution itself. How can we resolve this apparent contradiction? Clearly social and economic processes do not arise from nowhere, so we have to look for causes for them in the first place. However, once initiated, such processes can themselves contribute to further development through interaction and 'feedback'. Economic specialization, social stratification and the centralization of power all depend on a surplus economy, on the production of enough food to support not only those engaged directly in the production of food, but also those engaged in secondary industries, in trade or in administration. Granted this basis, which we know existed in southern Mesopotamia in the fourth millennium BC, we have seen how the nature of the subsistence economy, the development of technology and the importance of long-distance trade all contributed to the growth of economic specialization.

187

Social differentiation depends not only on the existence of a surplus but on the uneven distribution of this surplus in the community. This might arise in many ways. In southern Mesopotamia one reason for it was the uneven value of farming land, which led to a minority of the population holding the most valuable land. Another was the social value attached to certain occupations, such as those of merchants or priests, which meant that those holding them were expected to be well provided with material goods. Yet another reason was the 'fringe of private enterprise' which Frankfort discerned around the hard core of the State economy, which allowed enterprising individuals to supplement their 'State' (i.e. temple) allowance by the products of private commercial activities. Another likely cause is the third factor we are going to consider: the concentration of economic and political power in the hands of the temple authority. Those who were able to appropriate this power in the name of the city god, were in a position to appropriate also what wealth and privileges they wanted. The centralization of authority itself probably came about as a result of, among other things, the nature of the subsistence economy and the increasing economic specialization: a central authority became necessary to coordinate and control the increasing number of economic activities, and to manage the storage and redistribution of the food products, raw materials and manufactured goods produced by the new specialists.

The preceding paragraph is of course no more than a handful of comments on the social and economic structure, but it does indicate some ways in which processes of economic and social development, once initiated, can interact to produce further developments. Increasing economic specialization, increasing social differentiation and increasing centralization of power interacted to initiate a process of change that was irreversible (probably from the moment that economic self-sufficiency was abandoned) and in fact gained momentum until the Urban Revolution was fully accomplished. In terms of southern Mesopotamian cultural history we may see the process beginning in the Ubaid period, gaining momentum throughout the Uruk and protoliterate phases to culminate in the fully fledged (and relatively static) civilization of the Early Dynastic period.

Other factors

I have dealt here only with the main factors that were probably of relevance to the development of civilization. There may have been others. One I must mention here, though only to dismiss it as a major factor, is military activity. When a community faces a military threat from outside, a powerful force is exerted in favour of the development of a central authority, whose function in the first instance is military, but can be easily extended to cover other spheres of activity. Military leaders are frequently reluctant to abandon their power when the immediate threat has faded; both the

188

ancient and the modern worlds abound in examples of military dictators who came to power as popular war leaders, but who subsequently declined to step down in peacetime. Scholars often assign a major role to warfare in the emergence of Egyptian civilization, but it does *not* seem to have affected Mesopotamia at an early stage. It did become important later, during the Early Dynastic period, and was probably responsible for the emergence of kingship and the growth in power of the royal palace at the expense of the temple during the course of that period.

General discussion

Further archaeological work in the field and changes in fashion in theory will undoubtedly give rise to corresponding changes in emphasis in the importance assigned to the different factors that may have contributed to the accomplishment of the Urban Revolution. It seems unlikely, however, that any one of them can be discounted altogether or that any one can be considered of such overriding importance that it amounts to the sole cause.

In this final section I want to discuss three matters. The first is the relationship between Sumerian civilization and that of its contemporaries and successors in western Asia. In this we must tackle, if only briefly, the vexed question of diffusion versus independent evolution, which has plagued studies of early civilizations for so long. Secondly, I want to look at ancient civilizations in general, including those of the Americas, which undoubtedly evolved independently, to see how far the Urban Revolution in Mesopotamia was a unique process and how far it was paralleled in totally independent developments in different places at different times. Finally, I want to discuss the relevance of ancient Mesopotamian civilization to the modern world.

Sumer and civilization in western Asia

Archaeology has now established that civilization appeared earlier in southern Mesopotamia than anywhere else. Urban conglomerations of population, monumental architecture and writing were all in existence by 3500 BC, whereas they did not appear in Egypt for several centuries after this (and indeed we do not know of any Egyptian *cities* till much later still). In the Indus Valley even the Pre-Harappan or Early Harappan phase, with its small fortified towns, did not begin till shortly before 3000 BC and writing is not known before the mature Harappan phase which cannot be dated before 2500 BC. Sumer undoubtedly has the chronological priority and therefore it is *possible* that both the Egyptian and the Indus civilizations, as well as all the later civilizations of western Asia, were derivatives of Sumer. Here we must consider the evidence in favour of the view that civilization was diffused from this early centre and weigh it against the evidence for the independent development of civilization in different areas. I shall deal first with the two great civilizations of Egypt and the Indus Valley, and later with the smaller centres of urban life in western Asia, which pose a rather different problem.

Firstly I must make it clear that there is no question of Egyptian or Indus civilization being established by colonists from Sumer. There are no close similarities of culture of any kind; indeed it is hard to emphasize sufficiently the *differences* between these civilizations. What similarities exist are all on the conceptual level: the practice of irrigation agriculture, the existence of cities, of monumental art and architecture, of writing, the use of mud-brick and so on. The actual nature of the irrigation works, the form of the cities and their buildings and the nature of the written script are completely different in all three areas. Take the nature of settlement, for instance. In Sumer there were 15–20 large cities, each surrounded by smaller towns, villages and hamlets. In the Indus area, by contrast, there were two enormous metropolises and a host of smaller settlements, with no medium-sized towns in between. In Egypt we do not know of any cities of the early period, but the later pattern was one of a few major cities and both medium-sized and small settlements in between, arranged in this case in a linear pattern (imposed by the nature of settlement along the single valley of the Nile, in contrast to the pattern arising in the dual river system of Mesopotamia or the multi-river system of the Indus area). The cities themselves were very different too: the rigid, almost military looking layout of the Indus cities on their gridiron plan contrasts sharply with the higgledy-piggledy look of the Mesopotamian cities, with their winding lanes and their appearance of having grown up as circumstances required, without benefit of a preconceived town plan. Other differences abound. The writing systems provide an excellent example: the earliest writing in all three areas was basically pictographic, but the actual symbols chosen to represent a particular object were completely different. The art styles of the three civilizations are also totally dissimilar. It is indeed difficult to find any similarities at all, except on the general level mentioned above. Moreover there is remarkably little direct evidence for contact between the three civilizations, or, to be precise, between Mesopotamia and either of the others; for there is no evidence at all for contact between Egypt and the Indus. In Egypt there is evidence for contact with Mesopotamia in the period immediately before the First Dynasty (which began in about 3100 BC). The only actual imports that have been identified are three cylinder seals of late Uruk or protoliterate type. After this time the Egyptians used cylinder seals themselves (but as amulets, not as seals, for which they had no use as they did not use clay for writing), engraved with local designs, and their use is usually attributed to Mesopotamian influence. At the same time—in the late Predynastic period—Mesopotamian motifs

190

appeared in Egyptian art, including hunting scenes, boats that look like Mesopotamian craft and a scene with a hero subduing two lions rather like the motif of Gilgamesh and the lions which was so popular in Sumer. About the same time too appeared in Egypt a monumental style of building based on mud-brick, in contrast to the previous building style based on reeds, matting and palm branches. These Mesopotamian ideas were rapidly absorbed and the Egyptian civilization of the Archaic Period (3100–2700 BC) and the Old Kingdom (2700–2160 BC) shows no Mesopotamian features. Nor have any Mesopotamian imports been identified in Egypt at any time after the end of the Predynastic period.

The situation in the Indus Valley is different. As we have already seen, there is evidence of contact between the Indus area and Mesopotamia during the period of the mature Harappan civilization (c. 2500–1900 BC), which corresponds with the late Early Dynastic, Sargonid, Third Dynasty of Ur and Larsa periods of Sumer. However, this contact takes the form mainly of Indus manufactures in Mesopotamia: there are only a very few Mesopotamian objects in the Indus area and very slight hints of Mesopotamian influence in art motifs and in the appearance of a few cylinder seals. We have no evidence of anything comparable to the early appearance of Mesopotamian influence in Egypt in the period immediately *before* the crystallization of civilization; the contacts in the Indus area belong to the time of the fully developed civilization. However, as I have emphasized before, we know very little about the formative period of the Indus civilization and it is at least possible that further excavations might find traces of Mesopotamian influence at this time.

What does it all amount to? Henri Frankfort argued that in Egypt the Mesopotamian influence acted as a catalyst, speeding up a process of urbanization and civilization that was already under way. This view is accepted by many scholars today. Clearly the same idea could be applied to the Indus civilization; though we have no evidence of Mesopotamian influence during the crucial formative period, there obviously could have been contact, as we know there was later. Sir Mortimer Wheeler suggests that there was such influence. He writes: 'But ideas have wings, and in the third millennium the *idea* of civilization was in the air in western Asia. A model of civilization, however abstract, was present to the minds of the Indus founders'. How are we to evaluate this suggestion? It is not the kind of hypothesis that can be tested and cannot therefore be proved or disproved; it is rather a question of plausibility and acceptability to the individual. We know that there was Mesopotamian influence in Egypt at an early stage and that there could have been in the Indus Valley. What we are trying to assess is whether this influence played a major role in the development of civilization itself. We must ask ourselves what the Mesopotamians actually gave to the Egyptians and the population of the Indus Valley. The answer is—very little that we can put a finger on: the use of the cylinder seal almost certainly, and some art motifs; perhaps also a building style. But these things do not make a civilization or anything like it. They were not even important in the developing Egyptian and Indus civilizations. Cylinder seals were merely one form of amulet to the Egyptians, whereas in the Indus cities they occur only rarely and never competed with the local stamp seals. The art motifs were rapidly absorbed and had little or no visible influence on the development of local styles. The building style, if it was of specifically Mesopotamian derivation rather than of generalized west Asiatic origin, which seems more likely, again had little permanent influence: both Egyptian and Indus architecture has its own local and distinctive style. What we are left with is Sir Mortimer Wheeler's 'idea of civilization' and this to me is unconvincing. For the 'idea of civilization' is *our* idea: the brainchild of scholars of recent times, trying to make some sense of human history by processes of classification and generalization. The 'idea' of cities, the 'idea' of monumental architecture, the 'idea' of writing are all concepts that we have created in order to pull into some shape the amorphous mass of historical (and prehistorical) data we have to deal with. But the people of the fourth and third millennia BC would not grasp the 'ideas' of these things: they would see actual cities, real buildings and concrete examples of written documents. Surely they would not immediately abstract from these the general ideas that we see in them and go away and make *different* examples of them? If they were influenced by them, would they not make close copies? But this is exactly what we lack in the Egyptian and Indus civilizations; as I wrote at the beginning of this section, there are *no* close similarities with Mesopotamia. It seems to me that we are dealing with three fundamentally independent processes of the development of civilization in the alluvial valleys of the Nile, the Tigris-Euphrates and the Indus system. There were contacts between Mesopotamia and the other two areas but these had no more than peripheral influence, affecting some aspect of the style of the developing civilizations.

I must devote an additional paragraph here to the particular problem of writing. Many scholars have felt that the invention of writing was of such a special nature that it must have been invented once (in Sumer, because we know it appeared earliest there) and then spread to other areas. However, we have seen that the Egyptian and Indus scripts were totally different from that of Mesopotamia, not only from the developed cuneiform, but also from the earlier pictographic script. Thus, if the Egyptians and the Indus population acquired writing from the Sumerians, it was not an actual script they acquired, but the idea of writing. This is in fact the view propounded by many scholars today. However, it seems to me that the 'idea of writing' is a commonplace; it is the development of an efficient functional script that is the real achievement. Upper Palaeolithic man who scratched abstract symbols on pieces of bone (whatever they mean) had the 'idea of writing', as did his Mesolithic successor who painted signs on pebbles. What *they* lacked was any kind of social need for an organized system of writing. This appeared only with the development of complex economic and social organizations, which, as we have seen, was part of the Urban Revolution. When the need arose, the Sumerians, the Egyptians and the Indus population each in their turn invented writing to cope with it. The pictures and abstract signs that they were accustomed to using for decorative purposes were taken over and given standard conventional meanings—and a primitive script was born. Only in Mesopotamia do we see the script in its early primitive shape, but this is probably an accident of archaeological survival, arising from the different writing materials used in the three civilizations. With a little luck, we shall yet find early examples of Egyptian and Indus writing, showing the scripts in the process of formation.

So the Egyptian and Indus civilizations developed, I believe, to all intents and purposes independently of Mesopotamia. But what about the towns of the Persian Gulf, highland Iran and Afghanistan and Turkmenia? I have already suggested that towns arose in the first two areas as a result of the demand that arose in the great civilizations of the valleys for raw materials available in these coastal and highland areas. In this sense the towns of these areas were secondary, but they should not be regarded as simple derivatives of Sumer or the Indus civilization. There are two points that should be emphasized in this connection. The first is that none of these towns were colonies from Mesopotamia or the Indus Valley (in contrast to the Assyrian colony at Kultepe in Anatolia in the second millennium BC): they were local communities that took advantage of an opportunity to enrich themselves through exploitation of some of the demands of the great civilizations. The second point is that these communities had achieved a considerable level of social and economic development (though short of full civilization) *before* they became great towns through participation in trade with Mesopotamia and the Indus. Indeed it is probable that only fairly highly organized communities, at a level that we might describe as proto-urban, would be able to exploit the need for raw materials in Mesopotamia and the Indus Valley. The extraction, preliminary working and transport of raw materials such as lapis lazuli, steatite and metal ores requires a considerable personnel of skilled workmen, who must have been full-time specialists. Therefore only a community that could support a number of specialists not engaged in food production would be able to engage in trade on a considerable scale. The archaeological evidence indicates that the raw materials so much in demand in Mesopotamia and the Indus Valley had been discovered and exploited (though on a modest scale compared with the later development) by the local communities *before* the late fourth millennium BC when the Mesopotamian demand first became really active. Thus the rise of towns in the Persian Gulf and highland Iran and Afghanistan was due in part to local development which was then given an additional stimulus by the growth of trade in the raw materials needed by the great civilizations. As I suggested before, this explanation does not really apply to the development of towns in Turkmenia. It seems more probable that this area was another centre of independent development of urban life, although here the development never reached the level achieved in Mesopotamia, Egypt or the Indus Valley.

Towns elsewhere in western Asia which arose rather later, in the second millennium BC, were more obviously based on those of Mesopotamia. The Hittite towns of Anatolia, for instance, or the towns of the Levantine coast such as Ugarit and Byblos, although having a markedly local character, show many traces of Mesopotamian influence. For instance, Akkadian cuneiform was used in both areas (as well as local scripts) and the art styles in both evince many Mesopotamian characteristics; in the Levant, Egyptian influence was also apparent. And in western Iran, the Elamite civilization, which developed out of the Proto-Elamite cities described earlier, became *more* Mesopotamian in character as time progressed, finally adopting the cuneiform script in place of the earlier pictographic Proto-Elamite, though using it for the local language. These later civilizations of western Asia consciously borrowed many Mesopotamian practices and ideas and it is to them, especially to the Hittites and the Phoenicians, that we owe their survival and their transmission into our own culture.

Civilization in the Old World and the New

One of the questions that arises when we study the rise of the ancient civilizations of western Asia is whether this was a unique process (or series of related processes) or one that was repeated in essentials in different times and places. Was the development of Sumerian civilization a unique historical event or was it an example of an evolutionary process that man was bound or likely to follow? This essentially philosophical problem has concerned archaeologists and anthropologists for generations and extremes of both views have been adopted. While hyperdiffusionists claimed that all civilization had one origin (one school favouring Egypt as the cradle, another Mesopotamia), those who adopted a narrow evolutionary view of human history maintained that civilization was a stage of human development that all societies would eventually achieve. Neither of these extreme views has many adherents today, but the controversy is still very much a live one, if in a modified form. In the previous section I discussed this issue in relation to civilization in Mesopotamia, the Indus Valley and Egypt and came to the conclusion that the developments were more or less independent. However, this can be, and very often is, disputed and it is impossible to prove since we know that the areas were in contact with each other. The current trend—and it is a sensible one—in studying the development of civilization in general is to compare the Asian civilizations with those of the New World. No serious scholar today believes that any of the American civilizations had any connection with the Old World; they undoubtedly arose independently and can therefore be used as a 'control', with which we can compare the Old World development. This is not a matter I can discuss here in any detail—an adequate account of the civilizations of Mesoamerica and Peru would occupy a book at least as long as this one—but I shall mention briefly some of the similarities and some of the differences between the New World development and the Old, concentrating on the factors which I dealt with in my discussion of the rise of Mesopotamian civilization.

In the first place there was a significant similarity in the subsistence basis on which civilization grew in the two areas. New World civilizations were not based on irrigation agriculture, it is true, but they were based on the intensive cultivation of a cereal crop: in the Americas the native cereal was maize, which was first domesticated in Mexico but later spread to other areas. Civilization did not develop anywhere in the Americas where maize cultivation had not been adopted and become the basis of the economy.

In the Americas, as in Mesopotamia, marked population expansion preceded the emergence of civilization, and may have contributed to the process, unlike technological development, which is held by most scholars to have been incidental. I have already mentioned that the American civilizations lacked some of the important technological achievements of the Old World civilizations: none had ploughs, wheeled vehicles or sailing boats; some had no domestic animals or metal tools either. However, they were technologically in advance of their predecessors and of their non-civilized contemporaries and it is possible that technology played some role in the emergence of civilization—perhaps on the level of improving farming efficiency. Trade is also accorded a significant role in the development of civilization by some scholars, although in no area can it have been as important as in ancient Mesopotamia.

American archaeologists, who are generally trained as anthropologists, tend to concentrate on social factors in their analysis of the growth of New World civilization and here too there seem to be some valid parallels with the Asiatic civilizations. The growth of craft specialization, social stratification and the emergence of religious and political hierarchies with economic power were features of the American civilizations, as of the Old World ones and, in the same way that we discussed earlier, may have contributed to the accomplishment of the Urban Revolution itself.

These similarities are all on the conceptual level. The actual activities, institutions and processes took very different forms in the Old World and the New, as did the end products, the civilizations themselves. However, the similarities are there and we must not ignore them: in totally unrelated developments different societies underwent a somewhat similar process and arrived at a rather similar result, that we describe as civilization. Does this mean that we must return to the view held by the old evolutionary school, that civilization is a stage in man's development, towards which he will naturally move, and which he will eventually achieve? I think not, in the sense that the development is in any way inevitable. However, it does seem that the development of civilization is one of the cultural options open to man, given various environmental and other external opportunities. And it is an option that was certainly taken up by a number of societies in different places at different times.

Ancient civilization and the modern world

The development of civilization in western Asia is relevant to our own culture, not simply because it was an earlier, indeed the first, example of a process that was later repeated to produce our own society. The civilized communities of western Asia were in some ways, and via indirect routes, our own ancestors. It is now customary, and rightly so, to decry the idea that everything of importance came to Europe from the east—*ex oriente lux.* However, it is foolish to deny that European culture owes some debts to western Asia, both to the pre-civilized village societies that introduced farming (and the animals and crops that we still largely live on today) to Europe and to the civilizations themselves. Mesopotamian civilization itself survived until the last few centuries BC and through the third, second and much of the first millennia BC it exerted great influence on the neighbouring civilizations of Persia to the east, Anatolia to the north and the Levant to the west. And in their turn the civilizations of the Mediterranean, especially those of Greece and Rome which we recognize as our own cultural ancestors, borrowed much from the western Asiatic civilizations. This is not to say that classical civilization was not a new and vital creation, and indeed a distinctively European one, but many of its components were recognizably Near Eastern in origin and some are still recognizably so in our own culture. This is most noticeable in the sphere of religion: Judaism and Christianity are Near Eastern religions and they brought with them into Europe a mythology that is as old as civilization itself in western Asia, as we see from the Sumerian version of the Flood story. And even in the sphere that we claim as our distinctive achievement, that of pure science, it is difficult not to see a Mesopotamian ancestry. The Greeks may have invented pure mathematics, but it is doubtful whether they could have done so if the Sumerians and the Babylonians had not spent some three millennia making the manipulation of numbers a familiar and manageable activity. That we still divide the circle and the clock by the sexagesimal system used by the Sumerians and the Babylonians is positive testimony to the influence of Mesopotamia in this sphere. The alphabetic script we

New York—a city of the second millennium AD.

use is another Near Eastern trait, invented in this case not by the Mesopotamians but by some of their western neighbours in the late second and first millennia BC, the Phoenicians. I have selected just a few examples for this purpose, but they could easily be multiplied. I do not wish to claim that western civilization is in any direct sense the successor of the ancient west Asiatic civilizations. European civilization was fundamentally an independent creation and it absorbed influences from many areas other than western Asia. What I am claiming is that the earliest civilization in the world, that of Mesopotamia, had a lasting influence on society. It evolved a culture that lasted more or less intact for three millennia and contained elements that have survived for nearly as long again, until the present day. It is a very remarkable achievement.

Further reading

Bibby, Geoffrey   *Looking for Dilmun*, London, 1970

Daniel, Glyn   *The First Civilizations*, London, 1968

Hawkes, Jacquetta   *The First Great Civilizations*, London, 1973

Mallowan, M. E. L.   *Early Mesopotamia and Iran*, London, 1965

Masson, V.   *Central Asia*, London, 1972

Moortgat, Anton   *The Art of Ancient Mesopotamia*, London, 1969

Wheeler, Sir Mortimer   *Civilizations of the Indus Valley and beyond*, London, 1966

List of illustrations

from a seal of the Akkadian period. By courtesy of the Ashmolean Museum.

91 (above picture at bottom right) Impression from a seal of the Third Dynasty of Ur. British Museum. Photo: Werner Forman.

91 (bottom right) Impression from a seal of the Old Babylonian period. British Museum. Photo: Werner Forman.

91 (below left) Bronze cone bearing a foundation inscription. From the Temple of Nanshe at Sirare. *c.* 2100 BC. By courtesy of the Trustees of the British Museum.

95 (top left) Tablet bearing the laws of Eshnunna. Mid-2nd millennium BC. Iraq Museum. Photo by courtesy of the Press Office, The Embassy of the Republic of Iraq, London.

95 (right) Stele bearing the law code of Hammurabi. Mid-2nd millennium BC. Louvre.

101 Early Dynastic statuette of a man. From the Square Temple of Abu at Eshnunna. The Oriental Institute, University of Chicago.

103 (top) Impression from a seal of the Akkadian period depicting Gilgamesh and a lion. British Museum. Photo: Michael Holford.

103 (below) Impression from a seal depicting Gilgamesh and a boatman. *c.* 3000 BC. British Museum. Photo: Michael Holford.

109 (top) Silver lyre from the tomb of Pu-abi at Ur. By courtesy of the Trustees of the British Museum.

109 (below) Two of the four lyres found during excavation of the tomb of Pu-abi at Ur. By courtesy of the Trustees of the British Museum.

111 Predynastic marble head of a woman. From Uruk. Iraq Museum. Photo: Robert Harding Associates.

113 (top) Impression from a seal of the Jamdat Nasr period. British Museum. Photo: Werner Forman.

113 (centre) Stone cylinder seal. By courtesy of the Ashmolean Museum. Photo: Elsevier Amsterdam.

113 (below left) Impression from a seal of the Early Dynastic period. British Museum. Photo: Werner Forman.

113 (below right) Impression from a seal of the Akkadian period. British Museum. Photo: Michael Holford.

119 (top) The Citadel at Mohenjo-Daro. Photo: Robert Harding Associates.

119 (bottom left) Steatite seal depicting an elephant. From Mohenjo-Daro. Photo: The Mansell Collection.

119 (bottom right) Terra cotta model of a monkey. From Mohenjo-Daro. National Museum, New Delhi. Photo: The Mansell Collection.

128 (top) The Great Bath at Mohenjo-Daro. Photo: David Whitehouse.

128 (below) Oblique projection of the Great Bath at Mohenjo-Daro. By permission of the Archaeological Survey of India from *Mohenjo-Daro and the Indus Civilization* (1931) by Sir John Marshall.

133 Bronze statuette of a dancing girl. From Mohenjo-Daro. National Museum, New Delhi. Photo: The Mansell Collection.

138 (top) Terra cotta model of a buffalo. From Mohenjo-Daro. Photo: The Mansell Collection.

138 (centre) Terra cotta model of a ram's head. From Mohenjo-Daro. Photo: The Mansell Collection.

138 (below) Terra cotta model of an ox. From Mohenjo-Daro. Photo: The Mansell Collection.

146 Mountains in Kurdistan. Photo: Michael Mansell-Moullin.

149 (top) Painted bowl of the Susa A period. From Susa. By courtesy of the Ashmolean Museum.

149 (below) Painted beaker of the Susa A period. By courtesy of the Trustees of the British Museum.

153 (top) Steatite seal of the Dilmun culture of the Persian Gulf. Photo: P. V. Glob.

153 (below) Town wall at Qala'at al-Bahrain, Bahrain. 3rd/2nd millennium BC. Photo: P. V. Glob.

157 (top) Fragment of a clay tablet from Altyn-depe. 3rd millennium BC. Photo: Novosti Press Agency.

157 (below) Clay figurine of a woman, and a bowl. From Altyn-depe. Photo: Novosti Press Agency.

169 Aerial view of the mound of the prehistoric town of Jericho. Photo: © The Maison Photo Service, Los Angeles, California.

173 Tower in the town wall at Jericho. 7th millennium BC. Photo: Elsevier Amsterdam.

COLOUR PHOTOGRAPHS

Page

Index

204

crafts, Çatal Hüyük, 168–70; Indus Valley, 135–6; Iran, 151–2; Jericho, 168; Sumer, 76, 77–8; *79*; Susa, 147–8; Turkmenia, 156–8; Uruk culture, 176; *see also* art
cuneiform script, 19–24, 26, 42, 80, 85, 148, 154, 192, 194; *91*

Daily Telegraph, 24
Dales, George, 120
Dasus, 29
dating techniques, radiocarbon dating, 11, 14–15; tree rings, 14–15
'The Death of Gilgamesh', 72
Deh Luran, 163
dendrochronology, 14
Denmark, 8
Diakanoff, N. M., 54
Dilmun, 137, 152, 154, 155; *153*
divination, 90, 92, 100–1, 114
Diyala, 28, 37, 47, 112
Dumuzi, king, 43, 104, 107

economics, Sumerian, 53–5, 56, 59, 66
education, Sumerian, 90–3
Edzard, Otto, 55
Egypt, 10, 80, 177, 189, 190–2
Elam, 147; attacks Sumer, 43, 46, 107, 148–50; captures law code of Hammurabi, 93, 148–50; divination, 102; language, 20, 22; Sargon conquers, 45–6; trade, 78; *160*; writing, 194
Enki, 28, 42, 54, 59, 97, 104
Enlil, 54, 97, 99, 104
En-me-barage-si, king, 43
Enmerkar, king, 43, 104
Epic of Gilgamesh, 71
epic tales, Sumerian, 104–7
Erbil, *6*
Ereshkigal, 98
Eridu, 48, 54, 77, 97; *49*; and coastline of Persian Gulf, 34–7; excavations, 25, 28; royal palace, 68; temples, 41–2, 59–60, 61; *61*
Eridu culture, 175–6, 179
Eshnunna, 46, 47, 93; *49*
Euphrates, 10, 33, 34–7, 165, 172, 181
excavation techniques, 31

Failaka, 137, 154, 155
Falkenstein, A., 64
Flood, 11, 13, 14, 23–4, 104
Fox Talbot, William Henry, 22
Frankfort, Henri, 28, 30, 55, 56, 178, 188, 191

Ghaggar, river, 116
Gilgamesh, king, 43, 48, 104, 136, 191; *103*
Godin Tepe, 150
gods and goddesses, 54, 96–7, 98
Gordon, Cyrus, 20
Göttingen Academy, 20
granaries, Indus Valley, 127
grave goods, Indus Valley, 140; Iran, 151; Sumer, 71–2, 98; *70, 73*; Turkmenia, 158
Greece, 8, 10, 196
Grotefend, Georg Friedrich, 20
Gudea, 112; *106*
Guedinna, 90
Gula, 64, 99
Guti, 46

Hacilar, 164

Hajji Muhammad culture, 41, 42, 175, 179
Halaf culture, 41, 76, 175
Hamadan, 19
Hammurabi, king, 24, 46, 86, 89, 93, 94, 150; *95*
Harappa, 10, 11, 116, 122–5, 127, 130, 132; cemetery, 140; decline, 144–5; excavation, 29, 144; origins, 118–20; population, 134
Hassuna-Samarra culture, 41, 175
Herodotus, 112
Hilprecht, H. V., 25
Hincks, Edward, 22
Hittites, 10, 85, 102, 194
Hofuf oasis, 154
Homer, 19, 43, 104, 107
human sacrifice, 28, 72, 98
hymns and lamentations, Sumerian, 107

ideograms, 83–5; *84*
Im-dugud, 62
Inanna, 54, 60, 72, 97, 99, 104
Incas, 186
India, 8, 78
Indus, river, 172
Indus Valley, 10, 11, 116–45; archaeological discovery of, 16, 29; contacts with Dilmun, 154, 155; decline, 144–5, 161; Mesopotamian influences on, 191–2; origins of civilization in, 177, 189, 190, 191; trade, 80, 136–9, 158, 161
Iran, 11, 31, 41, 147–52, 162; archaeological discovery of, 16; cuneiform script, 19–22; decline, 161; origins of towns in, 193–4; trade, 78, 136, 151–2, 158; use of copper, 76; Ubaid culture, 180
Iraq, 162; *6*
Iraqi Directorate of Antiquities, 28
irrigation, development of, 30, 166; and development of civilization, 172, 177–8; Indus Valley, 134; Mesopotamia, 34, 37, 74
Ishtar, 97
Isin, 46

Jacobs, Jane, 8
Jacobsen, Thorkild, 37, 68
Jamdat Nasr (protoliterate phase), 114, 139; *49, 87, 111*
Jamdat Nasr culture, 41, 42, 180, 181
Jarmo, 164
Jericho, 164, 166, 167–8, 170–2; *169, 173, 174*
jewellery, Indus Valley, 135; Sumerian, 78; *36*
Jhukar culture, 131
Jordan, 164
Joshua, 167

Kalibangan, 120, 122, 124, 131, 145
Kanesh (Kultepe), 80, 86, 136, 193
Kassite dynasty, 148
Kathiawad, 131
Kermanshah, 19
Khafaje, 28, 47
Khuzistan, 41, 147, 163, 164, 166, 180
King Lists, 11–14, 28, 43–6, 48, 68, 90; *44*
kingship, Sumer, 66–72; *67*
Kish, 27, 43, 45, 48, 58, 68, 72, 83, 139, 181; *49*
Kluckhohn, Claude, 10
Konya plain, 171
Kot Diji, 120
Kramer, Samuel, 24, 54, 104, 114
Kroeber, A. L., 9

207

THE FIRST CITIES

105 illustrations (16 in full colour)

Towns of great complexity, brought to light in the last 150 years in Iraq and Iran and in Pakistan, have been dated back some 50 centuries. They were founded at a time when the rest of the early world, with the notable exception of Egypt, had mastered only the first principles of farming and could certainly not provide surpluses of food to keep a part of its population in urban conditions.

They were the centres of ancient Mesopotamia and the Indus Valley. They are epitomized by the metropolis of Ur and its magnificent royal tombs on the former course of the Euphrates, and by Mohenjo-Daro on the Indus. They are located and described by Ruth Whitehouse in an invigorating new account of an astonishing phenomenon.

Buildings and burials, public records and personal belongings and dozens more clues to everyday life make it plain that they enjoyed the 'civilization' of political and religious hierarchies, division of labour, burgeoning technology, codes of law and education, a flourishing import and export trade, music, arts and a written language. These towns were veritable cities, and the first in the world.

Ruth Whitehouse is a specialist in the prehistoric archaeology of Europe and the Near East.